# Higher Education, Fiscal Administration, and Budgeting

# Higher Education, Fiscal Administration, and Budgeting

## An Applied Approach

Gabriel R. Serna and Spencer C. Weiler

ROWMAN & LITTLEFIELD
*Lanham • Boulder • New York • London*

Published by Rowman & Littlefield
A wholly owned subsidiary of The Rowman & Littlefield Publishing Group, Inc.
4501 Forbes Boulevard, Suite 200, Lanham, Maryland 20706
www.rowman.com

Unit A, Whitacre Mews, 26-34 Stannary Street, London SE11 4AB

British Library Cataloguing in Publication Information Available

**Library of Congress Cataloging-in-Publication Data**
Names: Serna, Gabriel Ramon, author. | Weiler, Spencer, author.
Title: Higher education, fiscal administration, and budgeting : an applied approach / Gabriel R. Serna and Spencer C. Weiler.
Description: Lanham, Maryland : Rowman & Littlefield, 2016. | Includes bibliographical references and index.
Identifiers: LCCN 2016021489 (print) | LCCN 2016029535 (ebook) | ISBN 9781475825619 (cloth : alk. paper) | ISBN 9781475825626 (pbk. : alk. paper) | ISBN 9781475825633 (Electronic)
Subjects: LCSH: Education, Higher—United States—Finance. | Education, Higher—United States—Administration. | Universities and colleges—United States—Finance. | Universities and colleges—United States—Business management.
Classification: LCC LB2342 .S43 2016 (print) | LCC LB2342 (ebook) | DDC 378.1/06—dc23
LC record available at https://lccn.loc.gov/2016021489

∞ ™ The paper used in this publication meets the minimum requirements of American National Standard for Information Sciences—Permanence of Paper for Printed Library Materials, ANSI/NISO Z39.48-1992.

Printed in the United States of America

*For my wonderful husband, Dan*

—Gabriel

*I have been blessed to have seven loving parents in my life (biological parents, parents, stepmother, and in-laws). Each of these individuals has influenced me greatly—from choosing to put me up for adoption, to raising me, to loving me as if I were their own child. In particular, I wish to express my love and appreciation to my father, one of the greatest people I know. This book is dedicated to these seven amazing people.*

—Spencer

# Contents

# Foreword

I have been teaching a graduate-level course on the economics and financing of colleges and universities for twenty years. One of the difficulties I consistently encounter is finding a good, comprehensive source on issues of budgeting and finance. I can find recent chapters on the strengths and weaknesses of various budgeting systems and articles on the links between institutional planning and fiscal planning. However, finding one single source that brings all key aspects of institutional finance together has not been possible.

Drs Serna and Weiler have pulled together an impressive volume that covers all of the important topics for nonprofit higher education finance. Many students in higher education and student affairs programs have never been introduced to higher education finance and key budgeting terms. Indeed, they had never thought about the economics and finance of postsecondary education. In my classes I often say that the eyes of many senior administrators without a finance background start to *roll into the back of their heads during budget discussions.* Serna and Weiler start with an introduction to budgeting and key budgeting terminology. I am especially pleased that this volume includes a discussion of ratio analysis. These are key indicators of institutional fiscal health.

From here they go on to discuss revenue and expenditure patterns at universities and then move on to ratio analyses. This is the first book I have seen that discusses ratio analyses, and yet this is a key way to understand and examine the fiscal health of a college or university. I was particularly glad to see their chapter on the annual budget cycle and budget forecasting. This is important to understanding the ebb and flow of each fiscal year, and frankly these are topics I had not considered covering in my course—but I should have.

In sum, this is a first-rate resource for any higher education finance course. It brings together the latest thinking on all aspects of budgeting and finance into a single available source.

*Don Hossler*
*Professor Emeritus*
*School of Education*
*Indiana University Bloomington*

# Acknowledgments

We wish to express our appreciation to a number of people who have helped out immensely as this book developed from an idea to a reality. Luke Cornelius and Carlee Escue-Simon were instrumental in initiating this project and provided the original vision for this book. The book is decidedly better because of the inputs from two outstanding colleagues who reviewed the manuscript. Both David Tandberg and Nick Hillman did not hesitate to support this project, and both provided invaluable feedback that resulted in a better product. In addition, we would like to thank the HESA 696 class at the University of Northern Colorado for testing chapter materials and providing wonderful feedback. We are especially grateful to Andrea DeCosmo, who passed a careful eye over our equations and math. We also wish to thank Don Hossler for writing a wonderful foreword for the book. It is also necessary to thank Indiana University Bloomington, Virginia Tech, and the University of Pennsylvania for allowing us to use their public financial statements in our chapters and exercises. Finally, we wish to acknowledge the outstanding support of our colleagues, friends, and programs at Virginia Tech and at the University of Northern Colorado.

*Chapter 1*

# Introduction and Overview

In 1972 Liza Minelli and Joel Grey, in the movie *Cabaret*, popularized the familiar maxim "Money makes the world go round." This statement is particularly true in education. The purpose of this book is to help aspiring and new higher education budget managers appreciate the importance of money in operating a college, university, office, department, and program. Finances are at the core of virtually every decision made in higher education, and those leaders who develop the requisite skills to properly manage limited resources are better positioned to maximize the potential of each dollar.

Over the past decade, we, the authors of this book, have taught education finance and budgeting to aspiring educational leaders at two different institutions, and our shared experience has helped us to recognize that many of the students who enroll in our courses do so with a degree of trepidation. Most aspiring educational leaders are not attracted to the position by the prospects of managing a budget. However, the importance of proper fiscal administration is paramount.

It is our goal in our courses, and with this book, to not only stress the importance of finance and budgeting for aspiring educational leaders, but also demonstrate the required skills associated with properly managing money for the benefit of students and the larger goals of education. Indeed, we are convinced that the study of budgetary strategies is empowering and invigorating, and we hope to share this throughout this book with each reader. Ultimately, we will rate the success of our efforts with this book by the degree to which we are able to convince others of the confidence that comes with the knowledge of properly managing budgets within higher educational organizations.

The process of convincing the reader that managing a budget can be readily learned and applied begins with a brief discussion of the importance of money in higher education. Next, the focus shifts to the importance of budgetary skills for aspiring higher education and student affairs leaders. Finally, the chapter concludes with an overview of the organization of the book along with recommendations on how the reader should use it to increase his or her understanding of essential budgetary concepts, techniques, and strategies.

## THE IMPORTANCE OF MONEY AND THE LACK OF THEORY

One cannot overstate the importance of resources in higher education. Every decision made by leaders in higher education and student affairs takes into consideration the potential fiscal impact of that decision on the institution. In a simple phrase, money truly matters. A lack of resources restricts the actions that leaders can take to better support students. Conversely, an increase in resources affords leaders more options to better meet the needs of students.

A fiscal reality is that financial resources are limited. Increasingly, institutions are being asked to do much more, with much less. As a result, those entrusted with managing institutional budgets must possess the skills to reduce inefficiency, enhance effectiveness, and ensure that the limited budgets are used to maximize the educational benefits of all students. That is to say, much like other public-sector entities (Wildavsky, 1978), higher education must seek to be efficient, accountable, and effective in its mission and operations.

And while this may seem like a cut-and-dry process, the realities on the ground suggest otherwise. In fact, in public budgeting and financial management a major limitation has been the lack of a theoretical foundation to guide allocation decisions. And though economic theory has guided the behavioral aspects of decision-making, a truly budget-centered theory remains elusive. For example, as early as 1940, V. O. Key Jr. outlined how a lack of theory has led to "the absorption of energies in the establishment of mechanical foundations for budgeting," which has resulted in "diverted attention from the basic budgeting problem: on what basis shall it be decided to allocate $x$ dollars to activity A instead of activity B?" (p. 1138).

In other words, he states, as have others since then (Wildavsky, 1973), that fiscal administration, budgeting, and planning are decidedly human undertakings. The heavy focus on the mechanical processes underscored by Key (1940) likely points to the fact that it is difficult to adequately incorporate the human element into the decision to choose dedicating funds to activity A versus activity B from a purely budgetary perspective. Hence, fiscal administration has instead occupied itself with how to develop a budget proposal and a budget document and with forecasting and auditing financials.

Consequently, throughout the text, the intention is to stress the fact that budgeting and fiscal administration rely on the judgments of individuals working together. That is to say, resource allocation decisions and budgeting require human inputs, experience, and expertise to be done well. Though they rely on numbers, readers and new financial managers should not assume a blind objectivity to the process. Indeed, it is the human element that makes budgeting and fiscal administration both interesting and enjoyable.

The material contained in this book, along with the numerous activities geared to provide aspiring educational leaders with practical budget experience using real data, will help to develop those requisite skills related to technical competence and human judgment. Hence, not only does expertise matter, but so to does the efficient management of resources.

## THE IMPORTANCE OF BUDGET MANAGEMENT SKILLS

Leaders in higher education and student affairs seek the opportunity to lead for a myriad of reasons. Most of these reasons are centered on students and recognize the importance of a strong leader's influence over the establishment and maintenance of a safe learning culture for all stakeholders (students, faculty, staff, etc.). Few, if any, current higher educational leaders pursued formal leadership positions because they desired to manage, in some cases, multimillion-dollar budgets. And yet, ironically, in order for a leader to be effective in all other areas of the institutional governance process, this individual must be able to manage money.

One outstanding educational leader once stated, "The 'ances' will be the thing to get most people fired from administration—romance and finance." We do not want to see strong higher education leaders lose their ability to positively impact an institution due to preventable situations. We will leave the professional counseling related to romance in the workplace for others to explore and focus, instead, our ensuing discussion on the financial aspect of the job of fiscal administration in higher education.

Realizing that a majority educators entering into leadership positions lack formal training related to managing a budget, the contents of this book will address the importance of budget management in detail. However, for this chapter, the focus on the importance of proper budget management will be limited to overarching concepts. These concepts will be presented as questions:

• How do leaders decide which proposed revenues and expenditures to approve and which to reject?
• What do leaders do if the organization's expenditures exceed the revenues?
• How should leaders determine the benefit of current expenditures?

- What potential inefficiencies in a college, university, or unit can be eliminated without negatively impacting instructional practices and quality?
- Which budget approach should be used to allocate funds to departments, offices, programs, faculty, or other units?
- Is performance pay an effective way to improve the overall quality of instruction? Of research or of other areas?
- What are the different restrictions placed on the various funding sources available to institutional budget managers?

These questions begin to illustrate the importance for educational leaders to possess budgeting knowledge, and even expertise, in higher education. Our contention is that an educational leader who lacks strong budgetary knowledge when assuming a leadership position will experience a steep learning curve to get "up to speed," and this lack of knowledge could result in significant job-related issues. We have crafted this book to provide aspiring educational leaders with both an overview of the theoretical concepts related to budgeting and the opportunity to put the theoretical concepts into practice through an array of budgetary exercises.

## THE BOOK'S ORGANIZATION

This book is divided into four sections, which we are calling "phases" in the budgetary process. The focus of the first phase is on the foundational knowledge related to finance and budgeting that higher education budget managers should possess. There are four chapters included in this phase. The first of these has a discussion on the basics of budget and finance (chapter 2); the next deals with an exploration of revenues and expenditures in higher education (chapter 3), which is followed by an important study of financial ratio analysis (chapter 4) and forecasting (chapter 5).

The main focus of the second phase is on the steps that college and university budget managers must take to develop and oversee operating budgets for departments, programs, offices, or other units. This second phase contains two chapters. The budget cycle (chapter 6) is discussed in detail to ensure aspiring budget managers understand all of the steps involved in the process of developing and maintaining a budget in the higher education context. Next, the process related to overseeing, auditing, and analyzing the effectiveness of an existing budget (chapter 7) is explored.

In the third phase, we shift the discussion to capital budgeting. This phase is divided into two chapters. First, the discussion centers on funding capital projects without accruing debt (in the form of bonds) (chapter 8). Next, we explore the concepts related to funding capital projects while accruing debt (chapter 9).

The focus of the fourth phase is simply alignment. Ultimately, a higher education budget manager should ensure that spending practices align with the organization's vision statement, mission statement, goals, and strategic plan (chapter 10).

## PARTING THOUGHTS BEFORE GETTING STARTED

An interesting exercise is to ask standing higher education administrators which aspect of their jobs they felt the least prepared to take on when or if they graduated from a traditional higher education or student affairs administration program or when they started off in a position that required budget oversight. We sense that for a vast majority of current leaders, the answer will be related to budgeting. In addition, we would argue based on our experience that most aspiring educational leaders, when they start their graduate studies, lack a working understanding of higher education budgets.

Unfortunately, most preparation programs dedicate only a limited amount of time to exploring budgetary strategies; moreover, this exploration is done in a descriptive fashion, and the assumption is that higher education leaders will be taught, while on the job, how to properly oversee a budget.

We, obviously, feel this lack of attention to properly prepare aspiring educational leaders to create, manage, and oversee a higher education budget is dangerous and shortsighted. As a result, we wrote this book to support aspiring educational leaders and to provide those invested in preparing quality educational leaders for the twenty-first century with a tool that will bolster understanding of core budgetary theories and practices.

Our vision is that this book will aid in the development of higher education and student affairs leaders by instilling in these individuals a working understanding of the specifics of higher education budgets and of how to maximize the spending power of each dollar. For example, consider this question: What percent of inefficiency, or money poorly spent, is permissible in an institutional budget? Ideally, the answer would be "zero percent," but we are not sure that is realistic. So, the answer must be "as little as possible." We are certain that the concepts covered in this book will empower aspiring educational leaders to identify and work to eliminate inefficiencies and enhance effectiveness in higher education budgets.

Finally, any leader in higher education settings with a strong conceptual and practical understanding of how to create, manage, and oversee a budget will quickly discover the importance associated with this vital knowledge. This leader will be able to say "Yes" to innovative proposals, activities, or practices, which require funding and are aimed at improving the educational experiences of students due to the high efficiency of the budget as opposed to the leader who has to always say, "That is a great idea, but there isn't any money to make it happen."

## Phase I

# FOUNDATIONS

The first phase of this book will focus on the foundational knowledge an aspiring higher education budget manager and educational leader must possess in order to effectively manage the financial side of operations. Specifically, the reader will first explore revenues, where these dollars come from, and get a general sense of current patterns. In addition, the reader will learn about expenditures and what happens if expenditures exceed anticipated revenues. Finally, the foundational knowledge that aspiring college and university budget managers should possess includes the use of financial ratios and forecasting. These concepts will provide the novice higher education budget manager with the skills necessary to manage a budget in a way that provides useful information and decision-making support.

*Chapter 2*

# Getting to Know a Higher Education Budget

Yukl (2002, p. 2) analyzed a number of different definitions of leadership and then offered the following assessment: "Most definitions of leadership reflect the assumption that it involves a process whereby intentional influence is exerted by one person over other people to guide, structure, and facilitate activities and relationships in a group or an organization."

Leadership skills are essential for an educational organization to improve, and the dearth of leadership can negatively impact an organization for years. However, aspiring educational leaders rarely begin the journey of formal leadership training with a strong understanding of public budgeting. Instead, they demonstrate a prowess in other areas essential to leadership—interpersonal skills, motivation, vision, and so on—and the assumption is that the less innate skills, such as properly overseeing a budget, can be learned.

The irony in the current development of educational organization leadership is that aspiring leaders are typically required to complete one course in the area of finance and budgeting. Inevitably, graduates of higher education leadership programs are hired for positions when they lack all of the requisite skills to properly oversee large budgets in a way that allows these dollars to drive the organization toward improvement.

The purpose of this book is to supplement the theoretical training related to finance and budgeting and provide both aspiring and standing educational leaders with the opportunity to develop a working understanding of the budgetary process. Readers will be asked to "crunch numbers" throughout this book in an effort to transform theoretical concepts into real activities and, ultimately, to increase understanding.

The process of demystifying budgets for educational organizations begins with steps that can be taken to better understand a budget. This chapter is divided into four sections. The first section will explain why a budget is

essential to educational organizations. The second reviews different managerial approaches to allocating funds that educational leaders can utilize. The
third summarizes the revenue sources and allocations for higher education
organizations. The fourth explains the importance of educational leaders
developing a philosophy related to managing budgets.

## WHY BUDGETS?

One of the mysteries of life is that, regardless of a person's personal income,
*wants* almost always surpass revenues. We never seem to make enough
money to do all that we want to do. Against this backdrop, the answer to the
question "Why do I need to know about budgets?" should be clear. Higher
education organizations lack sufficient resources to do all they would like
to do, and a budget plays an essential role in ensuring that all of their *needs*
are funded. In addition, a well-crafted budget allows educational leaders to
prioritize *wants* so that the most pressing items are funded as well.

What are the needs in education? In higher education, the greatest budgetary *need* relates to personnel. Salaries can reach up to 70% of total institutional expenditures (Goldstein, 2012, p. 26). *Needs* would also include costs
associated with operations and maintenance of facilities, transportation,
police services, and debt service. However, *wants* are specific to each educational organization. For example, a university might *want* to gain access to a
different database for research purposes. In general, a budget enables educational leaders to maximize the potential of the limited resources they oversee.
What follows is a discussion on the purpose of a higher education budget.

### Higher Education Budget: The Purpose

The highly complex and multifaceted nature of the responsibilities encountered by colleges and universities require that institutions allocate resources
among a vast array of programs, departments, and offices. Moreover, the
nonprofit nature of these intricate organizations suggests a responsibility, not
only to those on campus, but also to the communities, states, and regions in
which they operate. It is in this environment that colleges and universities
must effectively articulate how resources can and will be allocated. It is at
the nexus of these concerns that the importance and purposes of budgeting
are highlighted. Without a clear plan, evaluating the diverse objectives of
colleges and universities would be chaotic (Goldstein, 2012).

In higher education, a primary concern for campus administrators is the
effective use of resources and the ability to generate sufficient resources
to support strategic and ongoing priorities. As a result, institutions must

carefully examine the level and types of resources available to achieve varied goals and mission.

The budgeting process is the manifestation of these activities. It is, in essence, the plan for the institution—the explicit means for understanding institutional priorities both historically and into the future (Goldstein, 2012; Rylee, 2011). It allows institutions to assess their efforts and to demonstrate that certain objectives and strategic endeavors have been effectively and efficiently supported (Goldstein, 2012).

In order for an institution to be effective, it must encourage comprehensive budgeting and planning so as to provide a framework or guide for understanding how programs, departments, and offices fit together; how objectives are developed and accomplished; and the role that faculty and staff play in this process (Kosten & Lovell, 2011). What is more, the budget allows institutions to carry out "what if" analyses (Rylee, 2011).

In other words, because colleges and universities operate under and within a number of internal and external constraints, the budget serves as a reference point. Administrators can use a budget to explore the impacts of possible decisions or external changes on resource generation and expenses. For those in higher education charged with day-to-day budget management duties, understanding the role and purposes of budgeting is vital, especially if leaders of particular activities, programs, departments, and so on are asked to provide evidence of effectiveness or to simply remain worthy recipients of institutional resources and thus remain operational.

## ALLOCATING BUDGET FUNDS

Once an organization (be it an institution, an office, or a department) receives funds, the leader, working collaboratively with a governing body, must take steps to allocate them into various budgetary categories. There are a number of ways in which leaders can approach the allocation of budgetary funds, and the most salient approaches are discussed here.

Budgeting approaches in higher education often reflect the processes undertaken in other nonprofit and public-sector organizations. Incremental and zero-based budgeting are typical approaches employed across a broad spectrum of public and not-for-profit organizations, including P-20 education. However, like school-based budgeting is more representative of P-12 education, certain approaches are more typical of higher education institutions. As a new budget manager, it is of utmost importance that one become conversant with the diverse array of possible approaches to budgeting in colleges and universities. These are briefly introduced and described here.

## Incremental Budgeting

Incremental budgeting takes the amount of money that was allocated to each subcategory in a budget during the previous fiscal year and reallocates that amount, with slight alterations to control for changes to the current fiscal year budget allocation, to the next fiscal year budget. For example, if a department received $1,500 for the previous fiscal year allocation and the institution's overall budget did not change at all for the next fiscal year cycle, then, under an incremental budgeting process, the department would receive the same amount or an incrementally adjusted amount based on organizational changes.

ADVANTAGES: Incremental budgeting is the least time consuming of all of the approaches discussed in this section. Moreover, it does not require that expenditure proposals be reviewed. Incremental budgeting is incredibly high on the efficiency continuum.

DISADVANTAGES: The most significant examples of misallocation of limited resources in public education typically occur under an incremental approach to allocating resources. Incremental budgeting diminishes the amount of supervision over proposed expenditures; however, there is still a degree of accountability. Finally, it encourages poor spending decisions when it is coupled with a "spend it or lose it" policy since people would rather make questionable spending decisions to ensure a similar budget in the future.

## Formula Budgeting

Although formula budgeting is typically used at the state or system-wide level, it is presented here so that new budget managers can become familiar with some of its key characteristics. While it is the case that incremental budgeting remains an important and primary budgeting approach in many states, as of 2007 at least eleven states report using formula budgeting as a primary approach (Pamley et al., 2009).

ADVANTAGES: Generally, this budgeting approach employs one or a number of formulas to determine the appropriate allocation of institutional resources based on program costs and demand. It is used primarily by public colleges and universities to guide institutional-level requests. Often, this approach is dependent on historical data or forecasted trends based upon enrollments and provides a rather simple way to make decisions.

DISADVANTAGES: While this approach offers a relatively simple, transparent, and quantitative measure to inform decision-making, it can also create significant difficulties, namely, that it tends to favor larger, more selective institutions and that the formula itself is vulnerable to political influences. It also creates incentives to continue programs that may not necessarily assist the institution in reaching its goals and accomplishing its mission because these programs contribute to the institution's bottom line. Finally, this approach lacks a mechanism for more micro-level evaluation of activities and programs, thus limiting its usefulness for intra-institutional decision-making (Barr & McClellan, 2011; Goldstein, 2012).

## Zero-Based Budgeting

Zero-based budgeting operates under the assumption that each budgetary category receives no money at the beginning of the fiscal year. Then, departments, offices, and programs are invited to submit expenditure proposals that will, ideally, be reviewed by the upper leadership team. This approach increases the transparency of the process and is essential for zero-based budgeting to effectively impact the allocation of resources. Those expenditure proposals that are deemed in alignment with the institution's vision, mission, and goals are approved, whereas those that do not align with the direction of the institution are denied.

ADVANTAGES: This allocation approach ensures there is no frantic rush to spend funds ineffectively at the end of the fiscal year to make sure those funds are not lost in future fiscal cycles. In addition, zero-based budgeting guarantees that approved expenditures are aligned with the focus of the college or university.

DISADVANTAGES: A disadvantage to zero-based budgeting is that it is time consuming. Some departmental, office, or program leaders may shy away from having to justify proposed expenditures and, as a result, may not even submit a proposal for review. In addition, denying proposed expenditures may create a culture of favoritism and mistrust within the institution (however, this final disadvantage can be significantly mitigated, if not completely eliminated, by a fully transparent decision-making process).

## Initiative-Based Budgeting

Under this budgeting model, the focus is on funding those activities that have been identified as strategic institutional priorities.

ADVANTAGES: This approach can take three common forms as outlined by Goldstein (2012, p. 101): (1) the institution captures a small to modest percentage of increased resources for a certain period and supports initiatives that have been established in the strategic plan; (2) set reallocation targets by unit such that each unit identifies those activities than can be eliminated or cut back to provide for their portion of the reallocation target; (3) use contingency funds included in the budget to fund the new initiative either in part or in full if the funds are not needed elsewhere to fill budgetary gaps. This approach allows departments, programs, and offices to meet their targets in a number of ways while helping to reach institutional or other goals using existing funding streams.

DISADVANTAGES: While a useful approach for new initiatives, this is not to suggest that there are no tradeoffs that accompany the use of this method. For example, much like formula budgeting, the planning process can favor certain programs or offices, and in some cases, these same groups may be funded only minimally, thus creating a larger burden on them when even small amounts are taken from their budgets. Clearly, this method of funding initiatives is more useful as a short-term means of providing resources for activities deemed to be central priorities. Therefore, it is important for the planning process to include a mechanism for funds to be returned to core activities at an appropriate time (Barr & McClellan, 2011; Goldstein, 2012; Varlotta, 2010).

## Performance-Based Budgeting

Performance-based budgeting involves resource allocation to particular inputs, activities, and outputs. Much like formula budgeting, this approach is often based at the state level, and therefore suffers from many of the same *advantages* and *disadvantages*, including the difficult nature of clearly linking aggregated performance measures with divisional and departmental objectives.

Additionally, because this method typically relies on measures promulgated by the state, it is not always apparent that important and influential factors are taken into account during the measurement development process. Moreover, the way in which the method is currently used means that only a small percentage of resources are impacted by this approach. Finally, although states have not typically penalized institution, for not meeting particular targets in terms of total appropriations, some states have begun to consider using performance-based budgeting to link state support to performance measures, including the use of stricter penalties (Barr & McClellan, 2011; Goldstein, 2012).

## Responsibility-Centered Management

Responsibility-centered management (RCM)[1] places budgetary authority and autonomy at the unit or program level.

ADVANTAGES: In this model each organizational unit is a revenue, cost, or combination center where the unit has ultimate control and responsibility for generating resources and covering costs. Revenue-generating units must pay cost centers for the services provided centrally. This allows for a great deal of autonomy at revenue center level.

For example, cost centers often include registrar services, library services, and physical plant space among others. The price of these services is frequently based on published state, federal, or association guidelines. These funds are then combined with the campus "tax" on unrestricted revenues generated by revenue centers and other central revenues (investment and endowment income, gifts, etc.) to form a pool of funds. This pool is then managed by the central administration to help support cost and revenue centers that operate at a deficit. This approach is attractive to unit administrators and deans because it sets resource allocation authority at the local level closer to where the "action" happens.

DISADVANTAGES: The approach is also limited because it places responsibility for shortfalls and year-end deficits squarely in unit administrators' and deans' purview as well. Still, those who support this approach suggest that its qualities include participation of campus-wide stakeholders, incentives for carefully evaluating costs and revenues, responsiveness to changes in the internal and external environment, and, finally, the ability to carry over budget surpluses from one year to the next. Although there are a number of positive elements to this method, there are additional disadvantages that should be highlighted.

For example, many detractors suggest that this model creates unhealthy competition and an inability to plan and budget comprehensively for the institution as a whole (Barr & McClellan, 2011; Goldstein, 2012; Kosten & Lovell, 2011; Varlotta, 2010). Additionally, the emphasis placed on the bottom line has been argued to adversely impact educational quality because "it promotes centers to choose the most cost-effective pedagogies, class structures, or course schedules over the most educationally purposeful" (Varlotta, 2010, p. 18).

Even, with the derision that this approach engenders, it has become the preferred budget approach in many institutions of higher education in both the public and private-sectors. As of 2005, at least eighteen private and ten public institutions employed this practice (Kosten & Lovell, 2011) and Goldstein (2012) provides evidence that it is, in fact, many more than that.

## Budget Hybrids in Higher Education

In this section we have presented a number of comprehensive budget models; however, it is unusual for an institution of higher education, or any public organization (Finkler et al., 2013), to use only one budget approach. Barr and McClellan (2011, p. 77) state that "hybrid models of budgeting are far and away the common mode of budgeting in higher education." Therefore, it is highly likely that new budget managers will encounter budget hybrids in their day-to-day work and are well advised to become conversant with the multitude of approaches available to them.

## MAJOR BUDGETING CATEGORIES

In nearly every facet of education budgeting and planning, a central concern for those charged with administering resources is the appropriate use of revenues and the efficient management and containment of expenditures. In order to effectively support strategic and core priorities, budget managers in education should become acquainted with the typical sources of revenues and expenditures that will help their institution to achieve its varied goals and objectives. In this section, we present the major resource and allocation categories faced by the sector.

### Revenues

In terms of revenue structure, institutions of higher education rely on a diverse array of sources. Table 2.1 outlines the major and most typical sources of revenue-generating activities undertaken by higher education institutions. As we suggest in the section on expenditures, the specificity of institutional budgets might differ from what is presented here. However, we believe that most institutional budget managers will find that the following section provides a pertinent outline for understanding the revenue side of a college or university budget.

As outlined in Table 2.1 public and private institutional revenues are derived from a number of sources; however, even this attempt at outlining the various types of revenues does not suggest that Table 2.1 presents a comprehensive list of possible revenues. As the landscape of higher education

**Table 2.1   Typical Major Revenue-Generating Activities of Higher Education Institutions**

| Revenue Source | Revenue Type |
|---|---|
| Student | Tuition and fees |
| Federal, state, and local government | Appropriations grants and contracts |
| Private | Gifts, grants and contracts, contributed services, church support, and royalties |
| Institutional endowment and fund balances | Investment earnings |
| Sales and services | Educational activities, auxiliary enterprises, medical services, hospitals, and independent operations (parking, library, and rental fees) |

*Sources*: Barr and McClellan (2011); Goldstein (2012); Serna (2013a); Toutkouskian (2001, 2003).

finance has changed, so too have the strategies employed by institutions to generate needed revenues in the face of declining state support, calls for accountability, and shifts toward more typically market-centered techniques for generating resources.

Tuition and fees remain vitally important to institutional finances. These revenues are generated from payments provided by students to cover a portion of educational expenses and do not include room and board, or other miscellaneous costs such as supplies (Toutkoushian, 2001, 2003). While a significant revenue source, tuition and fees also tend to be the most politically contentious and provide a central focus in policy debates—hence their importance to the budget manager (Barr & McClellan, 2012; Goldstein, 2012; Serna, 2013a).

Government funds include federal, state, and local government appropriations, grants, and contracts provided to institutions of higher education. These revenues include direct appropriations and funds for contracted services in addition to grants. They do not include Pell grants or direct student loans[2] (Toutkoushian, 2001, 2003).

Generally, state government appropriations are the single largest revenue source for institutions other than tuition and fees. However, the downward trend in this revenue source (Archibald & Feldman, 2006, 2011; Barr & McClellan, 2011; Cheslock & Gianneschi, 2008; Goldstein, 2012; Lowry, 2001; McLendon, Hearn, & Mokher, 2009; Serna, 2013; St. John & Priest, 2006; Tandberg, 2008) suggests that states will continue to decrease or hold steady funding as a proportion of overall institutional budgets even as enrollments are on the rise.

At most public research institutions, research is funded primarily by grants and or contracts or both (Barr & McClellan, 2011; Goldstein, 2012) from all sectors of government and industry. Often these revenue types cover the majority of the costs associated with the project. Though a useful and significant part of college and university revenue structures, the grant and contract revenues that universities receive from external funding sources such as a state or federal government are restricted to the project they support.[3]

Private gifts, contracts, and grants are those revenues that are provided privately, that is, by individual donors, corporate partners, church support, or other private entities. These revenues are aimed at supporting the three central institutional missions shared by most colleges and universities: teaching, research, and service (Toutkoushian, 2001). This revenue source also includes development[4] as it is commonly known. This category of private donations has grown significantly as public institutions seek alternative funding mechanisms (Cheslock & Gianneschi, 2008). Development is typically characterized by annual giving and long-term fund-raising campaigns to assist in supporting programs and various facilities (Barr & McClellan, 2011; Goldstein, 2012).

Investment earning are those revenues generated by the appreciation of an institution's endowment (Lerner, Schoar, & Wang, 2008; Toutkoushian, 2001) or by the investment of idle fund balances (Finkler et al., 2013). While they can provide a significant revenue stream, they are also vulnerable to economic variability. However, endowments play a central role in institutional finances, mission, and market perception (Kalsbeek & Hossler, 2008; Lerner, Schoar, & Wang, 2008). Revenue can also be generated from the investment of idle funds or fund balances.[5]

The use of fund balances to earn interest income is a simple way to generate small to modest income. An example would be staff salaries that are allocated yearly and which could be invested in secure short-term investment vehicles and withdrawn as needed, thereby generating income on otherwise idle funds. An important caveat to this strategy, however, is to avoid accounting problems by making certain that returns from the use of idle restricted funds used to generate short-term investment earnings are utilized for or returned to the same programs from which they originate.

Sales and services revenues are generally received from other educational activities, such as book store operations, food service, parking, and hospital operations. These revenues typically come from educational and auxiliary activities. In certain instances, institutions can choose to contract with external vendors who pay for the privilege to retain income streams from these operations to provide these services (Goldstein, 2012). However, before outsourcing these activities the costs and benefits of such a contractual arrangement should be carefully considered in addition to the considerations regarding the types of services that are appropriate for outsourcing (Kirp, 2003).

## Expenditures

As mentioned previously, colleges and universities have a diverse array of goals and objectives that are intended to help them meet institutional missions. To that end, institutions must expend resources to cover core and ongoing operations. In this section, we highlight some of the major expenditure categories budget managers encounter. In Table 2.2 a brief overview of expenditure sources and types is presented.

The goal is to help familiarize new budget managers in higher education with some of the primary ways in which most colleges and universities expend limited revenues. While it is the case, much like with revenues, that specific institutions might differ on some of the categories, most budget managers will find this section a helpful outline for basic understanding of the expense side of the budget.

**Table 2.2   Typical Major Expenditure Categories for Higher Education Institutions**

| Expenditure Source | Expenditure Type |
|---|---|
| Education and general activities (instruction) | Salary and benefits,* travel, equipment, software, and supplies |
| Research | Publications, programming, labs and equipment, professional development, internal and other sponsored programs, and memberships |
| Public service | Conferences, training, advisory services, extension services, and broadcasting |
| Academic, student, and institutional support services | Libraries, museums, cultural and social activities, student organizations, counseling, financial aid, registrar, executive and fiscal services, human resources, and planning |
| Scholarships and fellowships | Student financial aid (recognized as offsets to tuition and fees on the revenue side) |
| Mandatory and nonmandatory transfers | Contributions to system-wide operations, other transfers |
| Hospital and auxiliary enterprises | Medical school and clinics, bookstores, parking, student health, athletics, and other commercial entities |
| Physical plant, depreciation, and interest payments | Operation and maintenance, debt service, losses on sales of capital assets, and yearly physical assets charge |

*Sources*: Barr and McClellan (2011); Goldstein (2012); Toutkouskian (2001, 2003).
*Although salary and benefits are included in this category, the reality is that they are part of every category. Their inclusion in this category alone is because it is the central mission of most institutions of higher education and usually forms the largest category in terms of overall expenditures nearing on average a quarter of total salary and benefits costs.

Education and general (E&G) activities make up the single largest expenditure category for most colleges and universities. This budget category can range from an average of 25% at public four-year colleges to 38% at two-year colleges. These expenditures cover academic activities and the services supporting them directly, including primarily the instruction function.

Closely linked with expenditures on instruction are those aimed at supporting the research mission of most institutions. Expenditures in this category range from supporting the editorship of a journal by a faculty member to maintaining institutional memberships in particular associations or societies that help fill this part of the mission. This expenditure category also includes those funds expended for projects carried out by institutes, by centers, or by faculty under internal or externally funded grants and contracts (Toutkoushian, 2001; Goldstein, 2012). The expenditure amounts for this part of the budget are typically determined by the institutional mission and the emphasis placed on research. Still, we can think of no institutional type of nonprofit higher education, outside of community colleges, that does place at least some focus on research.

Turning to the third core expenditure category, public service, we find that this spending focuses primarily on the community-wide relationships maintained by the institution. As can be seen in Table 2.2, these activities include services to benefit the external community, including, for example, extension services, and, in many cases, public broadcasting (Toutkoushian, 2001; Goldstein, 2012).

The next two expenditure sources include those activities that focus on supporting the three primary missions of most institutions. Academic, student, and institutional support services (also known as general and administrative [G&A] expenses) provide much of the administrative infrastructure that allows colleges and universities to carry out day-to-day activities such as those listed in Table 2.2, in addition to many more that can be institution specific.

Scholarships and fellowships are aid provided directly to students. The primary distinction between these two aid types is that scholarships are commonly offered to undergraduates and fellowships to graduate students. This type of aid helps to defer some of the tuition costs faced by students. Therefore, it is important to note that, in order to avoid counting these two sources as both revenues and expenditures, most institutions recognize them instead as offsets to tuition and fee revenues. In other words, they are deducted from gross tuition revenue and are then counted as part of net tuition revenue in the budget[6] (Toutkoushian, 2001, 2003; Goldstein, 2012; Rylee, 2011).

While mandatory and nonmandatory expenditures do not necessarily help a single institution reach it objectives, these types of transfers can be understood to help a system do so instead. Transfers of this type are encountered by budget managers at public institutions that are part of a state's system and are intended as support for system-wide operations (Toutkoushian, 2001).

The last two expenditure sources are those associated with hospital and auxiliary services, and physical plant and depreciation. Hospital services are expenditures that are decidedly faced by those at four-year institutions. Expenditures in this category commonly include those that go toward covering the activities of teaching hospitals and medical schools as well as associated clinics.

Auxiliary services are those that operate separate from other institutional units such as parking and student health, for example. These units frequently operate on a fee-for-service model where auxiliaries are expected to generate enough revenues to cover their operating expenditures and oftentimes to cover capital costs. In some cases, an institution will decide to outsource some activities like those listed in Table 2.2; however, in these instances, it is not uncommon for the service provider to share some revenues with the institution and for the institution to charge the auxiliaries for services related to E&G (Toutkoushian, 2001; Goldstein, 2012). While often distinct from other auxiliary enterprises, some institutions include intercollegiate sports in this category as well (Goldstein, 2012).

Finally, the operation and maintenance (O&M) of physical plant space comprises a significant budgetary expenditure for institutions. These expenditures must cover upkeep, utilities, repairs, property insurance, and other items related to operating and maintaining the physical spaces in which college and university operations take place. A final major expenditure for institutions is depreciation for the physical plant and other capital assets. Depreciation includes the costs associated with the use of a capital asset during the current year. It allows an institution to pay for this asset over time instead of recognizing it all at once for operating budget purposes.

Because physical and capital assets require significant resources, large expenditures on these items are capitalized over the useful life of the asset. In the budget, only the cost associated with the use of the asset for the current fiscal year is recorded as an expense. These types of expenditures are closely tied to the operating budget because they impact the bottom line year to year. In the next section, we highlight some of the important relationships and distinctions between these budgets.

## OPERATING AND CAPITAL BUDGETS: BASIC DIFFERENCES

The basic distinction between operating and capital budgets is the timing of each. Operating budgets are those budgets that comprise the financial operations for the day-to-day functioning of the institution during a fiscal year, including revenues, reserves, and current expenditures. Conversely, capital budgets provide funding for new construction or significant facility renovations that take on a longer useful life (Goldstein, 2012). They play a significant role in covering long-term (more than one year) and major institutional expenditures, usually by issuing debt in the form of bonds.

The difficulty for institutions is understanding when, where, and how they can or should access this funding mechanism given the large amount of deferred maintenance many institutions face, especially in the public-sector. Barr and McClellan (2011) and Goldstein (2012) also remind universities of the impact the capital budget has on operating budgets. This is of vital importance given the fact that debt service (payments due on debt incurred) and depreciation costs become part of the operating budget, and thus operating expenses. Additionally, as new projects are brought online, they will create new revenue outflows as the institution begins to operate, outfit, and maintain them; these new costs will be reflected in the institution's operating budget in addition to debt service.

# PHILOSOPHY OF BUDGET MANAGEMENT

In previous sections we have covered a number of comprehensive approaches to budgeting and budgeting categories. In this final section the discussion turns to the philosophy underpinning the manner in which new budget managers might approach the task of actually administering the budget. Because institutions often have a long history of doing things in a particular way understanding, integrating, and possibly overcoming these practices and inertia are of significant importance for those becoming familiar with the budgeting process of a particular institution.

As a new budget manager in higher education and student affairs, a good place to start obtaining information may be by determining which budgeting approach the institution already employs. For example, certain budget approaches suggest a more centralized approach, such as incremental budgeting. However, approaches like RCM provide a much more decentralized approach to budget management. Regardless of the type of approach used institution-wide, some new budget managers might find that they are inclined to either a more or a less centralized budget administration process.

As with any management approach, there are positives and negatives associated with each course of action. Again, it is necessary to reiterate the notion that like budget approaches in general, a single, comprehensive method for overseeing budgets is unlikely. Most managers will develop a hybrid style that best reflects their philosophy of budget management and balances it with institutional or school needs and mission. As stated earlier, a hybrid approach to allocating revenues allows a leader to utilize the advantages of different approaches in an optimal manner. Educational leaders must never become too committed to one or two approaches to allocating resources. Instead, situational factors should contribute to the determination of the optimal allocation strategy.

Apart from the philosophical perspective taken by the budget manager, there are a few things that we suggest everyone should consider. First, the new budget manager should carefully examine the character of the institution. For example, what are the institution's goals, mission, short and long-term objectives, and how does the budget align with these state priorities? Additionally, what are the formal and informal mechanisms that undergird the resource allocation process and decision-making, and how does my management style fit into this process?

Second, a new budget manager should determine how transparent the process is. An important question that must be asked is whether the institution's character supports broad inclusion of individuals, units, programs, offices, and so on in the deliberation over resource allocation. Third, and closely related to this question is whether there exists a significant level of trust among stakeholders. If the budget process is opaque and trust is minimal, it is likely that an unhealthy climate will develop and will manifest itself in the budget process and final document. Again, the philosophical perspective taken by the budget manager can contribute positively or negatively to this process.

Fourth and finally, communication with budget units, other financial officers, and stakeholders around campus, at the main campus, or at other campuses should be of paramount importance. By communicating effectively and often throughout the budget process, the likelihood of distrust developing is diminished. The goal of the budget manager should be to help budgeting move along smoothly while keeping the community appraised of changes and to avoid surprises whenever possible (Goldstein, 2012). This course of action will help avert situations where distrust, gossip, rumors, or counterproductive behaviors arise.

The philosophical perspective taken by the budget manager should seek to encourage a culture of communication. In other words, share information and communicate, communicate, communicate!

## CONCLUSION

The purpose of this chapter was to provide the reader with a theoretical overview of a budget in higher education. This theoretical foundation related to a budget is essential as readers engage in the different activities incorporated in this book. All of the activities are aimed at taking theoretical components of working with budgets in an education setting and providing practical application. Ultimately, students of higher education budgets are encouraged to develop and refine their own budgetary philosophy.

## QUESTIONS ABOUT BUDGET BASICS AND ESSENTIALS

1. Why do we budget? What is the point?
2. What is the purpose of budgeting? How are budgeting decisions made in your unit, office, program, institution, and/or department? How does this relate to day-to-day activities?
3. Which budget approach do you think is the most useful? Why? Why are hybrid budget approaches becoming more popular? Do you know the approach that will be or is currently being used in your unit to make budgeting decisions?
4. What are the fundamental differences between operating and capital budgets? Why are they different?
5. Thinking broadly, how does budget philosophy of decision-makers matter in the budgeting process and for the fiscal administration as a whole?

## NOTES

1. This approach also goes by the names cost-center budgeting, profit center budgeting, and revenue responsibility budgeting (Goldstein, 2012).

2. The reason these are not included in this category is because these monies go directly to students and are therefore included as tuition and fee revenues.

3. While this revenue type is typically restricted to the grant or contract, it can become unrestricted, and thus included into the general operating budget, if funds are transferred to the operating budget as reimbursement for overhead and administrative costs, which add to overall institutional revenues.

4. Also known more generally as "fund-raising."

5. For a detailed explanation of this type of short-term investment, see Finkler et al. (2013).

6. Because the only amount noted on the expense side includes those monies paid directly to the student net of tuition and fees, Pell grants are not included in this category.

*Chapter 3*

# Revenue and Costs/Expenditure Structures in Higher Education

In educational contexts, for those charged with budgeting on a day-to-day basis, understanding the basics of revenue structure and generation is of central concern. Similar to their private-sector counterparts, budget managers and planners at colleges and universities must recognize the value of both anticipating revenues and revenue volatility based on contextual knowledge. While the specific revenue-generating activities differ for each institution of higher education based on its revenue structure, all institutions share similar structures. Therefore, in this chapter, the goal is to present the basic foundations for understanding revenue structures in higher education.

## SOME GROUNDWORK

Before starting with the nuts and bolts of the chapter, the presentation of a couple of very important ideas is necessary. First is the classification of expenses. In fiscal administration and budgeting, expenses can be ordered using *natural* or *functional* classifications. When they are grouped by natural classification, they refer to the purpose of the expense rather than to what it is meant to support. When classified by functional categories, expenses are related to the activities they support (Goldstein, 2012). Table 3.1 provides a basic distinction with some examples of expenses categorized by natural and functional classifications.

Second, it is important to mention the distinction of revenue into restricted and unrestricted categories. New fiscal and budget managers will quickly come to realize that certain revenues are restricted[1] to particular activities. Indeed, an important consideration in determining resource allocation is whether revenues are restricted to certain uses, offices, or projects. Moreover,

**Table 3.1    Example Expenses by Functional and Natural Classifications**

| Functional Classification | Natural Classification |
|---|---|
| Instruction | Compensation |
| Research | Benefits |
| Public service | Services |
| Academic support | Supplies |
| Student services | Utilities |
| Institutional support | Depreciation |
| Plant maintenance and operation | Scholarships |
| Student financial aid | Fellowships |
| Auxiliary services | |

*Source*: Goldstein (2012).

while total revenues may appear sufficient, in reality, decision-makers deal primarily with those portions of revenue that are unrestricted. Hence, special care must be taken when estimating the amount of total revenues and their allocation so that restricted funds are used appropriately.

## WHAT ARE REVENUES?

For the most part, total revenue is best understood as a relationship between *price* and *quantity* if employing typical finance and economic theory as a guide (Parkin, 2010). For example, in private firms that produce a measureable quantity of products or services, one simply needs to multiply the number of the good or service sold by its price to obtain the total revenues. This basic relationship is presented by the following equation:

$$Price \times Quantity = Total\ Revenue.$$

This equation makes perfect sense for estimating total revenues derived from countable quantities with easily measured benefits. However, the public nature of education at all levels can render this equation inappropriate for measuring total revenues. This is because the price of the "product" in education is not easily measured. Additionally, the quantity of the "product" in education is also difficult to estimate.[2] We delve into the particulars of these concerns in the next section on revenue categories.

### Revenues for Higher Education

Revenues for higher education institutions come from a variety of sources. Tables 3.2 and 3.3 provide a basic outline of the revenue categories of both public two- and four-year institutions; this is not to suggest, however, that

**Table 3.2   Operating Revenues for Public Four-Year Institutions in 2009**

| Revenue Category | Revenue Percent (%) |
|---|---|
| Tuition and fees | 19 |
| Local government | 4 |
| State government | 26 |
| Federal government | 14 |
| Auxiliary operations | 9 |
| Hospitals | 12 |
| Gifts | 4 |
| Other (includes capital appropriations) | 12 |

*Source*: Goldstein (2012, p. 57).

**Table 3.3   Operating Revenues for Public Two-Year Institutions in 2009**

| Revenue Category | Revenue Percent (%) |
|---|---|
| Tuition and fees | 17 |
| Local government | 20 |
| State government | 35 |
| Governmental capital appropriations | 4 |
| Federal government | 16 |
| Auxiliary operations | 4 |
| Gifts | 1 |
| Other (includes capital appropriations) | 7 |

*Source*: Goldstein (2012, p. 57).

these same categories are limited only to the public-sector. In institutions of higher education, revenues are typically derived from the seven to eight categories included in Tables 3.2 and 3.3. This breakdown is closely related to the institution's underlying mission. Although the categories reported here are for public institutions in 2009, the revenue categories themselves differ little for both the public and private-sectors in all but two categories.

For independent two- and four-year institutions, the percentage of revenues derived from tuition and fees were much larger at private two- and four-year colleges and universities (62% and 40% respectively), as compared to their public counterparts (19% and 17% respectively). In the second category, state support, private two- and four-year institutions derived only 4% and 1% of revenues respectively as compared to their public counterparts who received 35% of revenues for two-year colleges and 26% of revenues for four-year institutions (Goldstein, 2012). To help explain the each category in more detail, we provide basic definitions for each here.

According to Barr and McClellan (2011), Goldstein (2012), Serna (2013a) and Toutkoushian (2001), the following definitions apply to each revenue category:

1. Tuition and fees—Student payments for instructional services, which cover only a portion of costs incurred. This revenue type often accounts for a larger percentage of revenues at private institutions.
2. Local government—Funds appropriated by local governments to institutions. This revenue type is often more prevalent at two-year public institutions.
3. State government—Funds appropriated by state-level governments not including grants and contracts. Usually only appropriate to state-supported institutions.
4. Federal government—Funds appropriated to colleges and universities by the federal government, including those funneled through the state government, and do not include contracts or grants.
5. Auxiliary operations—Revenue derived from noninstructional services or goods and auxiliary enterprises. Housing is often considered an auxiliary service as are dining and parking.
6. Hospitals—Revenues derived from the operation of a university-affiliated hospital.
7. Gifts—Revenues from private donors. While this category does not include endowment income, the size of the endowment is closely related to the gifts an institution receives because gifts are often invested and resultant investment income is used to supplement certain operations related to the core mission.
8. Other—Revenues derived from other sources not shown in the tables. For this exposition, governmental capital appropriations are included here.

Turning to the calculation of total revenues, we mentioned at the beginning of this chapter that the typical total revenue equation for institutions is often inappropriate for colleges and universities. To illustrate, let us consider a more appropriate equation based on the revenue-generating activities cited by Goldstein (2012), Serna (2013a), and Toutkoushian (2001, 2003):

State Appropriations + (Tuition and Fees × Enrollments both FT and PT) + Other Revenue Sources – Institutional Financial Aid.

From this equation a few things become clear.

First, unlike the total revenue equation for private firms, the total revenue equation here does not presuppose that total revenues from state appropriations increase as quantity of students rise. In other words, state support, though enrollment-driven to some extent, does not necessarily reflect actual enrollments (Archibald & Feldman, 2011; Heller, 2006, 2011; Thelin, 2004). Hence, price and quantity in the previous equation do not share the same relationship as in Equation 3.1.

Second, while tuition and fees share a closer association with Equation 3.2, the ability to measure the total number of students is difficult given the realities of students stopping-out or dropping-out. Third, other revenues sources that matter a great deal for institutional budgets, such as investment earnings, grants, gifts, or contracts, may not be tied to the total number of students. Finally, an idiosyncrasy of higher education budgeting is the treatment of institutional aid or tuition discounts. In this case, revenues are offset to reflect institutional aid as revenue discounts that, nonetheless, reduce total available revenues.

This brief analysis has shown how the calculation of total revenues for colleges and universities introduces a great deal of complexity for fiscal managers. The goal, nonetheless, is to anticipate how these sources might change. For example, while student numbers rise, institutional budgets may not reflect a commensurate rise in revenues. Using techniques introduced in chapter 5, the objective then is to estimate with relative accuracy how certain fluctuations in any revenue source might impact the institution's ability to carry out its mission and meets its financial obligations.

Finally, revenues represent the foundation or the lifeblood of higher education. They drive all of the expenditures and programs and for this reason, aspiring budget managers must have a foundational understanding of the origins of revenues and how to properly forecast revenues for each budget year cycle.

## COSTS AND EXPENDITURES IN HIGHER EDUCATION

As noted previously, understanding the basics of organizational fiscal structure is of central concern to budget managers. While the previous section focused on understanding revenues, this section focuses on understanding expenditures and cost structures in higher educational contexts. Again, the public good nature of higher education means that for the most part fiscal administrators are working under a number of constraints. This requires that budget managers and planners at colleges and universities study expenditures and costs and understand fluctuations in this part of the fiscal structure. Additionally, the discussion here provides some nuance and delineation around different definitions and perspectives on costs and expenditures.

### What Are Costs and Expenditures?

As noted by Finkler et al. (2013), defining and measuring costs is highly complex. The reason for this complexity is related to the varied cost categories that exist. Here we present a number of costs that are typically included in the analysis of cost structures; however, please note that this list is not exhaustive. Also, the distinction between costs and expenditures has to do with expectations as related to spending, and actual spending.

Definitions of typical costs in higher education (Finkler et al., 2013; Goldstein, 2012):

1. Direct cost—Costs that are traceable back to the direct production of a good or service, or project or activity. In education instruction is often treated as a direct cost.
2. Indirect cost—Costs that are not readily traceable back to a project or activity, or to the production of a good or service. In education a typical example is physical plant maintenance or depreciation.
3. Variable cost—Costs that vary with the level of production of a good or service, or with volume changes in an activity or program. An example would also be instruction given that costs change directly as more instructors are hired or let go.
4. Fixed cost—Costs that do not vary with changes in the level of production of a good or service, or with volume changes in an activity or program. Again, physical plant would be a good example since the costs of the building is fixed, though maintenance might fall under variable costs.
5. Semi-variable costs—Costs that vary partially related to the productions of goods or services, or to changes in the volume of an activity or program. A prime example is student support services that employ physical plant for time periods after regular working hours. Regular working hour utility costs are relatively fixed; however, the use of buildings after this time means higher utility rates based on hours used.
6. Marginal cost—These are the costs incurred for providing one more unit of a good or service. For example, adding one more student to a course.
7. Average cost—This cost calculation is obtained by dividing the full costs associated with the production of a good or service, or activity or program by the number of individuals served. One example might be a tutoring program. For this instance, the total costs of the program are divided by the number of participating students.

As can be seen from these basic definitions, the measurement of costs is clearly difficult. However, our goal here is to simply highlight the ways in which costs can be understood and how these definitions can help budget managers more fully grasp the nuance of cost analysis. Finally, we should highlight that throughout this chapter we use the words "cost," "expense," and "expenditure" interchangeably when presenting information on the cost side of the fiscal structure for educational organizations.[3]

# TYPICAL OPERATING EXPENSES IN HIGHER EDUCATION

In institutions of higher education, costs are typically made up of eleven or twelve expenditure categories listed in Tables 3.4 and 3.5 based on institutional mission and size. It should again be highlighted that although the categories reported in these tables are for public institutions, the expenditure categories themselves are very similar across both the public and private-sectors in all but one category. For independent two-year institutions, the percentage of expenditures dedicated to institutional support nearly equals the amount spent on instruction (29% and 34% respectively), whereas for two-year publics that amount is only 14% (Goldstein, 2012). To help elucidate the significance of this comparison we provide some basic definitions of each category.

**Table 3.4  Relative Operating Expenses for Public Four-Year Institutions in 2009**

| Expenditure Category | Expenditure Percent (%) |
|---|:---:|
| Instruction | 27 |
| Research | 12 |
| Public service | 5 |
| Academic support | 7 |
| Student services | 4 |
| Institutional support | 8 |
| Physical plant maintenance/operation | 6 |
| Depreciation | 5 |
| Student aid | 3 |
| Auxiliary operations | 9 |
| Hospitals | 12 |
| Other | 2 |

*Source:* Goldstein (2012, p. 68).

**Table 3.5  Relative Operating Expenses for Public Two-Year Institutions in 2009**

| Expenditure Category | Expenditure Percent (%) |
|---|:---:|
| Instruction | 38 |
| Research | 1 |
| Public service | 2 |
| Academic support | 8 |
| Student services | 9 |
| Institutional support | 14 |
| Physical plant maintenance/operation | 9 |
| Depreciation | 5 |
| Student aid | 8 |
| Auxiliary operations | 5 |
| Other | 3 |

*Source:* Goldstein (2012, p. 68).

Drawing again from definitions provided by Barr and McClellan (2011), Goldstein (2012), and Toutkoushian (2001), each cost/expenditure category can be understood as follows:

1. Instruction—Known as educational and general activities (E&G), this expenditure category includes costs related directly to instruction and its related administrative costs such as faculty salaries.
2. Research—Expenditures related to both sponsored (external) and institutionally (internal) funded research activities.
3. Public service—Expenditures related to the provision of institutional services to external groups such as public broadcasting.
4. Academic support—Expenditures related to the previous three categories that help support the institutional mission. Good examples include libraries and museums.
5. Institutional support—Known as general and administrative (G&A) expenditures, these costs include nonacademic administration activities such as executive administration, accounting, or human resources.
6. Physical plant operation/maintenance—Expenditures related to upkeep and renovation of institutional buildings or facilities. As noted by Toutkoushian (2001), expenses related to the acquisition of a new building are not typically included here, but rather in the capital budget.
7. Depreciation—Those charges related to the use of physical assets such as buildings that have limit to their use but are expected to be in operation for more than a single year.
8. Student aid—Aid provided to students from all sources, including institutional, state, local, private, and federal, other than Pell grants. For aid provided by the institution this aid is typically not treated as an expenditure but rather as a tuition discount and thus is included on the revenue side of the budget.
9. Auxiliary operations—Typically, expenditures are related to fee-based activities and are self-supporting while not being directly related to the institution's core mission such as dorms and dining.
10. Hospitals—Expenditure related to the operation of a university-affiliated or university-run hospital.
11. Other—A category of expenditures that are unrelated to other standard operating activities.

As can be seen in Tables 3.4 and 3.5, institutional mission matters a great deal for expenditure patterns across higher education. We again wish to highlight the importance of the underlying managerial and budget philosophies as well as institutional goals and plans to the allocation of resources in educational context. While budget and managerial philosophies may not directly impact the percentage of expenditures in each category, they are certainly related to how these costs are spread among units or offices.

Moreover, institutional goals, and the planning that outlines how these goals will be met, can serve to solidify a certain course of action reflected in the percentage of the budget spent for each category, or in the case of revenues generated by each category. In this same vein, the planning process can also serve as a means for reframing the institution's strategic position and hence, require a realignment of expenditures or revenues to match these goals.

The aim of this chapter has been to shown how cost measurement for colleges and universities is highly intricate and therefore creates some important implications for anticipating costs and expenditures. For fiscal administrators in any sector, the goal is not only to forecast costs, but also to understand, based on both local knowledge and historical data, how these costs might vary into the future.

For example, we noted earlier that at private two-year institutions, institutional support was nearly equal in percentage terms to instruction. Based on this information, an institution may wish to reexamine it organizational structure and, as a result, its cost structure. A good budget manager will be able to provide forecasts that again help decision-makers anticipate the "what ifs" (Rylee, 2012) of certain decisions. For public-sector institutions, decreasing state support means that institutions are now operating in a more volatile fiscal environment.

That is to say, while revenues derived from state sources are dropping, costs appear to be on the rise. Budget managers should be able to provide some sense of how expenditure patterns can or should change based on the financial conditions faced by institutions. A stark reality in the current finance of public higher education is the long-term viability of colleges and universities in an environment characterized by decreased public support and increased accountability. For educational leaders, being able to "pay the bills" is of utmost importance, and having good data, good information, and sound analytic capacities can help alleviate some of the uncertainty related to both internal and external fiscal fluctuations.

## CONCLUSION

As noted earlier, external and internal forces can have an effect on both the revenue side and cost and expenditure structures of higher education institutions. Additionally, the consideration of multiple scenarios where worst- and best-case scenarios are studied applies to both sides of the budget. Strong fiscal administration requires valid and appropriate data and providing reasonable estimates, hence, the importance of the budget manager's local knowledge and know-how regarding the overall fiscal structure of an institution.

This discussion sets the foundation for the next chapter on forecasting. Whereas our focus in this chapter has been on revenues and costs/expenditures, the techniques introduced in the next chapter are useful for any type of forecasting. While we state this in the next section, we wish to once again underscore the fact that well-trained, well-informed budget managers provide the needed foundation for successful fiscal administration. In terms of forecasting, it is often the intersection of budget philosophy with contextual information that makes forecasts useful to decision-makers.

## QUESTIONS REGARDING EXPENSES, COSTS, AND REVENUES IN HIGHER EDUCATION

1. How is the calculation of revenues in higher education different from that of most other entities? Why is this the case?
2. How are costs different from expenditures? Please provide a couple of examples of these differences.
3. How have the major revenue/expenditure categories in higher education changed? Why has this shift occurred?
4. How is institutional mission related to revenue and expenditure patterns and reliance?

## NOTES

1. Though expenditures/expenses can also be restricted, they generally derive this categorization from their relationship to a restricted revenue source.

2. While the nuance of this notion is outside of the scope of the current chapter, readers can obtain further information on this topic from Winston (1999) and Parkin (2010).

3. In accounting practice and in some governmental organizations, these definitions can mean very different things. For a detailed discussion, we suggest reading Finkler et al. (2013). Still, the basic understanding is that costs relate to a functional relationship between production and provision of goods and services, whereas expenditures, or expenses, are actual dollar amounts.

*Chapter 4*

# Basics of Financial Ratio Analysis

The foundational elements of financial ratios and how to use them are the main foci of this chapter. In the fiscal administration of institutions, ratios can provide much needed information and evidence about their financial standing and fiscal viability. To help frame this in the day-to-day activities of budget managers, this chapter covers only the most typical ratios used in higher education and provides a step-by-step approach for understanding how to analyze and interpret the data conveyed by financial ratios, as well as their limitations.

## FINANCIAL RATIOS

Broadly speaking, financial ratios provide information about four areas of fiscal administration and budgeting:

1. Resource liquidity and flexibility
2. Debt capacity, leverage, and management
3. Asset performance and management
4. How an institution uses and obtains its funds (Chabotar, 1989; Prager, McCarthy, & Sealy, 2002).

These four areas arguably compose the major financial structures of the institution. By employing financial ratios across these areas it is possible to obtain a broad, summative understanding of the institution's fiscal positioning. Before moving ahead, a few definitional explanations are in order. Regarding the use of certain nomenclature for financial reporting, it is necessary to point out the conventions used for nonprofit-sector entities.

Typically nonprofit entities, including public and private colleges and universities, use a financial reporting style that mirrors that of public agencies. This means that as compared to the corporate/private-sector, different names are employed for financial statements and reporting elements within these statements. For example, because nonprofits do not generate profits, any excess between revenues and costs is considered to be a *fund balance*, which is also used in higher education.

In the same vein, a balance sheet in the corporate finance sector is called a *statement of financial position* in the public-sector, including private, nonprofit institutions. In public higher education, it is typical to find this information under the *statement of net assets*. Examples[1] of each type are presented in Figures 4.1 and 4.2.

Information on operating activities, often called a statement of operations in corporate finance, usually goes by the title *statement of revenues, expenses, and changes in net assets* at public institutions and by *statement*

(in thousands)

| | June 30, 2008 | June 30, 2007 |
|---|---|---|
| **Assets** | | |
| Cash and cash equivalents | $    735,340 | $    739,660 |
| Accounts receivable, net of allowances of $10,800 and $10,463 | 157,557 | 138,674 |
| Patient receivables, net of allowances of $103,518 and $105,633 | 293,304 | 250,090 |
| Contributions receivable, net | 445,064 | 379,422 |
| Loans receivable, net of allowances of $2,947 and $2,994 | 188,324 | 94,155 |
| Other assets | 117,089 | 134,007 |
| Assets held for sale | 3,902 | 6,835 |
| Investments, at fair value | 6,578,921 | 7,307,482 |
| Plant, net of depreciation | 3,479,761 | 3,067,833 |
| Total assets | $ 11,999,262 | $ 12,118,158 |
| **Liabilities** | | |
| Accounts payable | $    186,023 | $      90,411 |
| Accrued expenses and other liabilities | 958,389 | 905,593 |
| Collateral due broker | — | 495,893 |
| Deferred income | 120,280 | 78,052 |
| Deposits, advances, and agency funds | 140,838 | 132,049 |
| Federal student loan advances | 77,823 | 77,247 |
| Accrued retirement benefits | 342,618 | 293,226 |
| Debt obligations | 1,327,144 | 1,333,060 |
| Total liabilities | 3,153,115 | 3,405,531 |
| **Net assets** | | |
| Unrestricted | 4,466,107 | 4,273,780 |
| Temporarily restricted | 2,101,245 | 2,313,624 |
| Permanently restricted | 2,278,795 | 2,125,223 |
| | 8,846,147 | 8,712,627 |
| Total liabilities and net assets | $ 11,999,262 | $ 12,118,158 |

**Figure 4.1   Example *Statement of Financial Position* Used by Private Colleges and Universities.** *Source:* Edited by Authors, Public Records: Multiple Institutions.

| Assets | | |
|---|---|---|
| **Current assets** | | |
| Cash and cash equivalents | $ 671,293 | $ 552,892 |
| Accounts receivable, net | 111,087 | 107,947 |
| Current portion of notes and pledges receivable | 14,199 | 13,295 |
| Inventories | 13,021 | 11,724 |
| Short-term investments | 46,735 | 43,601 |
| Securities lending assets | 81,219 | 63,600 |
| Other assets | 34,265 | 27,686 |
| Total current assets | 971,819 | 820,745 |
| **Noncurrent assets** | | |
| Accounts receivable | 13,445 | 14,772 |
| Notes and pledges receivable | 63,173 | 66,770 |
| Investments | 915,008 | 714,836 |
| Capital assets, net | 2,316,762 | 2,197,123 |
| Total noncurrent assets | 3,308,388 | 2,993,501 |
| **Total assets** | 4,280,207 | 3,814,246 |
| Liabilities | | |
| **Current liabilities** | | |
| Accounts payable and accrued liabilities | 231,074 | 205,363 |
| Deferred revenue | 151,319 | 139,630 |
| Current portion of capital lease obligations | 1,149 | 1,242 |
| Current portion of long-term debt | 60,848 | 51,172 |
| Securities lending liabilities | 81,219 | 63,600 |
| Total current liabilities | 525,609 | 461,007 |
| **Noncurrent liabilities** | | |
| Capital lease obligations | 2,600 | 2,730 |
| Notes payable | 31,168 | 11,457 |
| Assets held in custody or others | 74,334 | 67,958 |
| Deferred revenue | 62,874 | 40,097 |
| Bonds payable | 848,205 | 749,181 |
| Other long-term liabilities | 58,550 | 64,255 |
| Total noncurrent liabilities | 1,077,731 | 935,678 |
| **Total liabilities** | 1,603,340 | 1,396,685 |
| Net assets | | |
| Invested in capital assets, net of related debt | 1,555,422 | 1,475,395 |
| Restricted for: | | |
| Nonexpendable - endowments | 19,399 | 19,088 |
| Expendable | | |
| Scholarships, research, instruction and other | 114,316 | 92,627 |
| Loans | 25,067 | 24,239 |
| Capital projects | 10,115 | 16,595 |
| Debt service | 6,300 | 5,162 |
| Unrestricted | 946,248 | 784,455 |
| **Total net assets** | 2,676,867 | 2,417,561 |
| **Total liabilities and net assets** | $ 4,280,207 | $ 3,814,246 |

**Figure 4.2 Example *Statement of Net Assets* Used by Public Colleges and Universities.**
*Source*: Edited by Authors, Public Records: Multiple Institutions.

*of activities* at private nonprofit colleges and universities as presented in Figures 4.3 and 4.4.

Both in higher education and corporate finance, a statement of cash flows, as shown in Figures 4.5a and 4.5b, includes information regarding the cash generated under the areas of operations, noncapital financing,[2] capital financing, and investment activities.

Finally, unlike the corporate sector, public entities, including higher education institutions, do not have shareholders and as a result do not report a

| (in thousands of dollars) | Fiscal Year Ended | |
| --- | --- | --- |
| | June 30, 2010 | June 30, 2009 |
| **OPERATING REVENUES** | | |
| Student fees | $ 1,088,373 | $ 985,888 |
| Less scholarship allowance | (170,091) | (133,054) |
| Federal grants and contracts | 318,646 | 295,737 |
| State and local grants and contracts | 23,830 | 28,860 |
| Nongovernmental grants and contracts | 102,839 | 127,049 |
| Sales and services of educational units | 64,475 | 61,498 |
| Other revenue | 181,640 | 175,506 |
| Auxiliary enterprises (net of scholarship allowance of $18,750 in 2010 and $15,850 in 2009) | 323,571 | 332,586 |
| **Total operating revenues** | 1,933,283 | 1,874,070 |
| **OPERATING EXPENSES** | | |
| Compensation and benefits | 1,684,964 | 1,632,926 |
| Student financial aid | 150,779 | 125,830 |
| Energy and utilities | 64,031 | 65,447 |
| Travel | 36,930 | 40,397 |
| Supplies and general expense | 430,712 | 449,435 |
| Depreciation and amortization expense | 125,715 | 120,819 |
| **Total operating expenses** | 2,493,131 | 2,434,854 |
| **Total operating loss** | (559,848) | (560,784) |
| **NONOPERATING REVENUES (EXPENSES)** | | |
| State appropriations | 549,755 | 572,578 |
| Grants, contracts, and other | 99,613 | 63,304 |
| Investment income | 103,265 | (17,607) |
| Gifts | 78,049 | 76,181 |
| Interest expense | (32,401) | (31,829) |
| **Net nonoperating revenues** | 798,281 | 662,627 |
| **Income before other revenues, expenses, gains, or losses** | 238,433 | 101,843 |
| Capital appropriations | 3,005 | 10,248 |
| Capital gifts and grants | 17,323 | 19,980 |
| Additions to permanent endowments | 545 | - |
| **Total other revenues** | 20,873 | 30,228 |
| **Increase in net assets** | 259,306 | 132,071 |
| Net assets, beginning of year | 2,417,561 | 2,285,490 |
| **Net assets, end of year** | $ 2,676,867 | $ 2,417,561 |

**Figure 4.3   Example of *Statement of Revenues, Expenses, and Changes in Net Assets* for Public Institutions.** *Source*: Edited by Authors, Public Records: Multiple Institutions.

statement of shareholders' equity in their financial reports. With this information, it is now possible to turn to an explanation of the uses of financial ratios.

## Uses of Financial Ratios

There are, generally speaking, four specific questions that should guide the use and interpretation of financial ratios:

1. Are resources sufficient and flexible enough to support the mission?
2. Does asset performance and management support the strategic direction?

| | Unrestricted | Temporarily Restricted | Permanently Restricted | 2008 | 2007 |
|---|---|---|---|---|---|
| **Revenue and other support:** | | | | | |
| Tuition and fees, net | $ 681,801 | | | $ 681,801 | $ 638,143 |
| Commonwealth appropriations | 49,674 | | | 49,674 | 49,429 |
| Sponsored programs | 744,862 | | | 744,862 | 736,343 |
| Contributions | 85,590 | $ 59,377 | | 144,967 | 127,870 |
| Investment income | 153,941 | 122,508 | | 276,449 | 271,948 |
| Hospitals and physician practices | 2,814,753 | | | 2,814,753 | 2,619,941 |
| Sales and services of auxiliary enterprises | 101,013 | | | 101,013 | 96,789 |
| Other income | 210,780 | | | 210,780 | 181,100 |
| Independent operations | 68,188 | | | 68,188 | 63,782 |
| Net assets released from restrictions | 198,777 | (198,777) | | | |
| | 5,109,379 | (16,892) | | 5,092,487 | 4,785,345 |
| **Expenses:** | | | | | |
| Program: | | | | | |
| Instruction | 909,962 | | | 909,962 | 847,491 |
| Research | 584,775 | | | 584,775 | 592,225 |
| Hospitals and physician practices | 2,588,374 | | | 2,588,374 | 2,361,208 |
| Auxiliary enterprises | 115,162 | | | 115,162 | 111,813 |
| Other educational activities | 160,063 | | | 160,063 | 153,233 |
| Student services | 48,775 | | | 48,775 | 46,397 |
| Support: | | | | | |
| Academic support | 62,066 | | | 62,066 | 60,807 |
| Management and general | 198,287 | | | 198,287 | 190,233 |
| Independent operations | 63,361 | | | 63,361 | 60,214 |
| | 4,730,825 | | | 4,730,825 | 4,423,621 |
| Increase (decrease) in net assets before nonoperating revenue, net gains, reclassifications and other | 378,554 | (16,892) | | 361,662 | 361,724 |
| Nonoperating revenue, net gains, reclassifications and other: | | | | | |
| (Loss) gain on investment, net | (153,228) | (191,085) | $ (24,401) | (368,714) | 920,744 |
| Investment income, net of amounts classified as operating revenue | (24,541) | (62,554) | 1,310 | (85,785) | (59,649) |
| Contributions | | 119,952 | 176,663 | 296,615 | 233,502 |
| Pension and other postretirement plan adjustments | (70,258) | | | (70,258) | |
| Income from discontinued operations | | | | | 394 |
| Net assets released from restrictions | 61,800 | (61,800) | | | |
| Increase (decrease) in net assets before cumulative effect of change in accounting principle | 192,327 | (212,379) | 153,572 | 133,520 | 1,456,715 |
| Cumulative effect of change in accounting principle | | | | | (67,490) |
| Increase (decrease) in net assets after cumulative effect of change in accounting principle | 192,327 | (212,379) | 153,572 | 133,520 | 1,389,225 |
| Net assets, beginning of year | 4,273,780 | 2,313,624 | 2,125,223 | 8,712,627 | 7,323,402 |
| Net assets, end of year | $ 4,466,107 | $ 2,101,245 | $ 2,278,795 | $ 8,846,147 | $ 8,712,627 |

**Figure 4.4** **Example of *Statement of Activities* for Private Institutions.** *Source:* Edited by Authors, Public Records: Multiple Institutions.

3. Do operating results indicate the institution is living within available resources?

4. Is debt managed strategically to advance the mission? (Prager, McCarthy, & Sealy, 2002, p. 5)

By considering these four questions, decision-makers are better able to determine the best ways in which to allocate resources to meet institutional objectives, goals, and mission. Indeed, Chabotar (1989) suggested that ratio analysis provides a means for answering these questions. This is because financial ratios provide a gauge, or metric, for understanding whether the

| *(in thousands of dollars)* | Fiscal Year Ended | |
|---|---|---|
| | *June 30, 2010* | *June 30, 2009* |
| **CASH FLOWS FROM OPERATING ACTIVITIES** | | |
| Student fees | $ 917,302 | $ 857,522 |
| Grants and contracts | 470,505 | 429,288 |
| Sales and services of educational activities | 63,915 | 66,624 |
| Auxiliary enterprise charges | 331,501 | 329,765 |
| Other operating receipts | 184,325 | 183,746 |
| Payments to employees | (1,661,635) | (1,621,284) |
| Payments to suppliers | (523,649) | (566,558) |
| Student financial aid | (154,558) | (128,528) |
| Student loans collected | 8,231 | 15,563 |
| Student loans issued | (5,287) | (8,073) |
| **Net cash used in operating activities** | **(369,350)** | **(441,935)** |
| **CASH FLOWS FROM NONCAPITAL FINANCING ACTIVITIES** | | |
| State appropriations | 549,755 | 584,501 |
| Nonoperating grants and contracts | 99,613 | 63,304 |
| Gifts and grants received for other than capital purposes | 80,592 | 74,276 |
| Direct lending receipts | 584,784 | 512,207 |
| Direct lending payments | (584,813) | (512,031) |
| **Net cash provided by noncapital financing activities** | **729,931** | **722,257** |
| **CASH FLOWS FROM CAPITAL AND RELATED FINANCING ACTIVITIES** | | |
| Capital appropriations | 3,005 | 10,248 |
| Capital grants and gifts received | 18,456 | 6,922 |
| Purchase of capital assets | (244,778) | (254,898) |
| Proceeds from issuance of capital debt, including refunding activity | 180,073 | 73,766 |
| Principal payments on capital debt, including refunding activity | (49,909) | (50,075) |
| Principal paid on capital leases | (1,464) | (1,906) |
| Interest paid on capital debt and leases | (45,850) | (45,718) |
| **Net cash used in capital and related financing activities** | **(140,467)** | **(261,661)** |
| **CASH FLOWS FROM INVESTING ACTIVITIES** | | |
| Proceeds from sales and maturities of investments | 2,633,797 | 1,500,824 |
| Investment income | 72,718 | 27,114 |
| Purchase of Investments | (2,808,228) | (1,568,213) |
| **Net cash used by investing activities** | **(101,713)** | **(40,275)** |
| **Net increase (decrease) in cash and cash equivalents** | **118,401** | **(21,614)** |
| Cash and cash equivalents, beginning of year | 552,892 | 574,506 |
| **Cash and cash equivalents, end of year** | **$ 671,293** | **$ 552,892** |

Figure 4.5a  Example *Statement of Cash Flows* for Higher Education Institutions. *Source*: Edited by Authors, Public Records: Multiple Institutions.

institution is positioned to answer each of these questions in the positive. Even if decision-makers answer these questions in the negative, financial ratios can help them determine where problems and obstacles exist.

In addition, financial ratios provide information to external stakeholders. Especially in the case of public higher education, state policymakers are introducing more complex accountability, performance-based, and over-sight mechanisms, which are often accompanied by requests for increased data and information (Hillman, Tandberg, & Gross, 2014; McLendon, Hearn, & Deaton, 2006; Tandberg & Hillman, 2014). Moreover, credit

| (in thousands of dollars) | Fiscal Year Ended | |
| --- | --- | --- |
| | June 30, 2010 | June 30, 2009 |
| **RECONCILIATION OF OPERATING LOSS TO NET CASH USED IN OPERATING ACTIVITIES:** | | |
| Operating loss | $ (559,848) | $ (560,784) |
| Adjustments to reconcile operating loss to net cash used in operating activities: | | |
| Depreciation and amortization expense | 125,715 | 120,819 |
| Loss on disposal of capital assets | 4,487 | 4,175 |
| Changes in assets and liabilities: | | |
| Accounts receivable | (7,091) | (72) |
| Inventories | (1,297) | (2,223) |
| Other assets | (6,579) | (5,947) |
| Notes receivable | 2,722 | 6,251 |
| Accounts payable and accrued liabilities | 25,249 | (9,303) |
| Deferred revenue | 34,466 | (7,071) |
| Assets held in custody for others | 6,376 | 1,381 |
| Other noncurrent liabilities | 6,450 | 10,839 |
| **Net cash used in operating activities** | **$ (369,350)** | **$ (441,935)** |

**Figure 4.5b**   *(Continued)*.

rating agencies such as Moody's, Fitch's, and Standard & Poor's carefully examine many of these ratios when determining bond ratings (Fischer et al., 2004; Serna, 2013b).

In public and private higher education, concerns around the costs of higher education are also significant (Archibald & Feldman, 2008, 2011; Serna, 2015). Financial ratios are a simple way to provide information regarding the fiscal standing of an institution and generate a quick measure of whether it is employing its resources appropriately related to its stated mission, vision, and goals. However, an important cautionary note is required here: while these measures afford a quick snapshot look at an institution's finances, as with any and all other data used for decision-making, financial ratios should be understood in context and with appropriate restraint.

Now that the fundamental uses of financial ratios have been presented, the focus of the next section is on the types of financial ratios budget managers in higher education are likely to encounter.

## TYPES AND INTERPRETATION OF FINANCIAL RATIOS

There exist a multitude of financial ratios across finance and financial management. However, for nonprofit higher education institutions, a few of these matter a great deal for gauging fiscal standing. In order to employ financial ratios, it necessary to have at least a few pieces of information. First is to know which ratio to use. In other words, what is being measured or needs to be reported?

Second, one must know where to obtain the required values from. Does the analyst or manager know where these data live? Third, one must know how to interpret the results of the calculation. Is this value too high? Too low? Should the goal be to increase/decrease this value? In the sections that follow, this is outlined in a step-by-step manner, which is then cross-referenced with the four areas mentioned earlier in this chapter.

Drawing upon a number of sources (Chabotar, 1989; Finkler et al., 2013; Fischer et al., 2004; Prager, McCarthy, & Sealy, 2002), the following sections introduce the basic elements of financial ratio analysis by separating them into four general areas. While a number of alternatives exist to the ratios presented here (see Prager, McCarthy, & Sealy, 2002; Fischer et al., 2004), these ratios provide a foundational understanding of financial ratios for the new fiscal administrator.

## Liquidity Ratios

The goal of liquidity ratios is to determine the financial strength of an institution's cash flows and whether the entity has sufficient cash to meet current and short-term obligations. These ratios rely upon the current assets and liabilities, or quickly cash-convertible assets and quickly due liabilities, or liabilities due within a year's time. Typically, one would go directly to the *statement of financial position* for private, nonprofit institutions, and to the *statement of net assets* for public institutions.

In most cases, current assets and liabilities are clearly indicated within the statement. In others, they are not. To help with this inconsistency, the typical assets and liabilities included in the calculation of liquidity ratios are identified in Table 4.1. In the instance that the required data are not reported separately, an understanding of the local context coupled with technical know-how come into play. The fiscal manager can always request for information that is not readily apparent on financial reports produced for public consumption.

As a quick aside, it is important to note the distinction between restricted and unrestricted assets and liabilities. Similar to restricted and unrestricted revenues discussed later in this chapter, assets and liabilities that fall into

**Table 4.1   Typical Current Asset and Liabilities**

| *Current Assets Types* | *Current Liability Types* |
|---|---|
| Cash and cash equivalents (checking balances, petty cash, etc.) | Accounts payable |
| Accounts/notes receivable | Deferred revenues |
| Short-term investments | Current debt service |
| Inventories | Current capital lease service |
| Prepaid expenses | Accrued leave (unused leave balances) |

restricted categories are limited in their use. That is to say, restricted assets and liabilities are only available and payable with monies from the specific activity or asset class. Typically, those liabilities resulting from the use of restricted assets are the same ones associated with the acquisition of restricted assets. They are also those liabilities that are expected to be liquidated using restricted assets (Hegar, 2015).

The most common of liquidity ratios is referred to as the *current ratio* (Chabotar, 1989, p. 193; Finkler et al., 2013). The current ratio is illustrated in the following formula:

Current Ratio = Unrestricted Current Assets/Unrestricted Current Liabilities.

The word "current" indicates the inclusion of assets that are quickly trans-formable, within a year or less, to cash. A similar notion applies to current liabilities. These are expenses that are required to be paid within a year. Typically, the goal should be to maintain a *current ratio* of 2:1 or simply 2. What this indicates is that for every dollar of current liabilities, the institution has $2 in current assets. Anything much lower than the 2:1 ratio is likely to draw unwanted, and negative, attention from creditors. In addition, a ratio lower than 2:1 could signal that cash reserves are being depleted (Chabotar, 1989; Finkler et al., 2013).

And while it might seem like a good idea to have a higher ratio in this case, a current ratio that is higher than 2 implies that the approach for determining and forecasting current cash needs is overly conservative, which could result in a loss of investment income if these funds were instead properly invested in short-term vehicles. While the current ratio provides a quick measure of liquidity, it can also mask cash flow problems when an institution is able to transfer funds from other areas. Although these two actions would postpone liquidity problems, they will not work over the long term (Chabotar, 1989; Finkler et al., 2013).

The next measure of liquidity is called the *quick ratio*. This ratio is espe-cially useful for institutions that maintain large inventories of some type such those related to bookstores, medical centers, and so on. The quick ratio does a better job of accounting for the role of inventories in the establishment of fis-cal standing since it removes these assets from *Unrestricted Current Assets*. In order to measure the quick ratio, the following equation is used:

Quick Ratio = Unrestricted Current Assets–Inventories/Unrestricted
Current Liabilities.

Because this ratio takes a more conservative approach to the estimation of current assets, a ratio of 1:1 or 1 is acceptable. Again, the larger the ratio, the more important it becomes to examine cash forecasting assumptions, discussed later in the text, to make sure that funds are not sitting idle. Conversely, if the ratio is closer to zero, this could suggest a real cash flow problem, and an examination of current spending or resource allocation decisions should take place.

A third liquidity ratio, referred to as the *available funds ratio*, is a more conservative measure of an institution's liquidity. This ratio limits the inclusion of current assets to cash and short-term investments and is represented in the following equation:

$$\text{Available Funds Ratio} = \text{Cash and Short-Term Investments/Unrestricted Current Liabilities.}$$

In the available funds ratio, only assets deemed to be liquid are included in the numerator. Given that this measure is even more conservative than the quick ratio, it is acceptable for this ratio to be as low as 0.75:1 or 0.75 cents of highly liquid assets to every dollar of current liabilities. Using this extremely conservative measure allows an institution to truly understand the cash position of the organization since the included assets are limited to those that are near cash equivalents (Chabotar, 1989).

## Operating Performance Ratios

The ratios included in this category typically measure the flexibility of institutional resources as well as whether or not an institution is "living within available resources" (Prager, McCarthy, & Sealy, 2002, p. 22). In order to obtain the necessary information for the calculation of these ratios, one should look to the *statement of revenues, expenses, and changes in net assets* or the *statement of activities* and in the case of *use* ratios to departmental or office budgets directly.

Typical operating revenues, expenditures, and nonoperating revenues are presented in Table 4.2. However, before moving forward, a few caveats are again in order. First, as noted by Toutkoushian (2001, p. 17), "Variations in account practices across institutions could result in the same expenditure item being grouped into different categories." Not only does this hold true for expenditures, but the same could be applied to revenue variables. Therefore, the information reported in Table 4.2 should be used only as a guide for understanding the respective components of operating performance ratios.

It is possible to report using either functional classifications—budget or natural classifications. While the same overall information is provided, this decision means that categories can differ based on local reporting norms.

**Table 4.2 General Operating Categories and Included Elements by Functional Classification**

| Operating Revenues | Operating Expenses | Nonoperating Revenues |
| --- | --- | --- |
| Tuition and fees | Student financial aid | State appropriations |
| Federal grants/contracts | Instruction | Gifts |
| State, local grants/contracts | Research | Investment income |
| Nongovernmental grants/contracts | Public service | Nonoperating grants/contracts |
| Sales and services | Academic support and student services | |
| Auxiliary enterprises | Operation of plant | |
| Scholarship allowances* | Depreciation | |

*Sources*: Serna (2013a); Toutkoushian (2001, 2003).
*As noted in chapter 3, it is an idiosyncrasy of higher education that scholarship monies can be treated as revenue discounts; hence, this value is a negative one but is removed from the revenue side as opposed to added to expenditures.

For example, a natural classification of expenses in Table 4.2 would include compensation and benefits, energy and utilities, travel, and so on rather than the functions they support.

A reminder of the information covered in chapter 3: revenues can be categorized into restricted and unrestricted categories. For the budget manager, this means maintaining clear oversight of which funds are available for general use and which are restricted to only specific uses. Because restricted funds (revenues or assets), and often any income derived from these funds, can only be used for certain purposes, using these numbers in the calculation of both liquidity and operating ratios should take into account the special character of restricted fund and asset classifications, especially since they include such categories as debt service and scholarship monies.

Two general ratios employed to measure operating results and flexibility include the *net operating ratio* and *expenditures by program or function ratio*. The *net operating ratio* is usually calculated using some combination of net operating revenues divided by total revenues, or total unrestricted revenues[3] (Chabotar, 1989; Fischer et al., 2004, p. 133; Prager, McCarthy, & Sealy, 2002), and takes the form:

Net Operating Ratio = Operating Revenues−Operating Expenses/Total (Unrestricted) Revenues.

When interpreting this ratio, a general approach is to determine if the ratio returns a result that is above or below 1.0. If the result is below 1.0, this indicates a deficit. If it is above 1.0, this indicates a surplus (Chabotar, 1989). An important caveat is necessary at this juncture.

For public institutions, it is not unusual to show an operating loss. This is because, as noted in chapter 3, operating revenues are decidedly connected to those revenues derived from the general operations undertaken by an entity. In public higher education, part of the operating budget comes from state support through nonoperating[4] related revenues. Hence, if the calculation just presented is used, it will always return a ratio of less than 1.0. A way to get around this limitation is for public institutions to present a ratio of total revenues to total expenditures (Chabotar, 1989) as follows:

Revised Net Operating Ratio = Total Expenditures/Total Revenues.

To illustrate, assume that a public institution calculates the difference between its operating revenues and operating expenditures and the result is $244,796. If this is compared to, say, $780,743 of operating revenues only, then the *net operating ratio* would be equal to 0.313, suggesting that the institution consistently has fund deficits. If, instead, the comparison is made between total expenditures and total revenues, then the example, including nonoperating revenues, would result in a situation where, for example, total expenses equal $1,025,539 and total revenues include the $780,743 of operating revenues and $324,169 of nonoperating revenues, the ratio changes to approximately 1.08.

Clearly, this second calculation is a better indicator of the financial net operations of a public institution. Additionally, it should be underscored that if the ratio is below 1.0 for one year, this is not necessarily a problem. Concerns should arise, however, around a trend where the net operating ratio is less than 1.0 for more than a couple of consecutive years, if deficits are characteristic of more than two of the most recent five years, or if there is a deficit larger than 10% of total revenue in any single year or more (Chabotar, 1989, p. 199).

The next operating ratio to consider is the *expenditures by program or function ratio*. As will be noted in chapter 10, coupling the expenditure by program or function ratio with the organization's strategic planning, fiscal administration, and budget alignment provides a clear measure of institutional priorities over and above any plan. The ratio is calculated using the following information (Chabotar, 1989, p. 198):

Program or Function Ratio = Expenditures by Program or Function/Total Expenditures.

Rather than provide a strict range of values, this ratio measures the total resources expended on a particular program or function. This type of ratio is especially useful for offices and departments that wish to understand how the institution's resources are being expended. This ratio is also useful in helping to determine the relative position that stated goals and objectives, as well as offices and departments, maintain in allocation decisions. For example, if total expenditures are equal to $1,025,539 and student aid expenditures are equal to $17,237, then the percentage of the budget dedicated to this office/program is less than 2% (1.68%).

It could be argued that if this is considered a strategic priority, the budgetary expenditures on this area do not seem to fit the rhetoric. Another example could look at an institution that wishes to become more research oriented. Using the same example, if total expenditures are $1,025,539 and research expenditures are $271,550, then the percentage of the budget dedicated to research is about 26.5% (26.47%). This is nearing one-third of institutional expenditures on this function and, therefore, would probably indicate a true dedication to this part of the strategic plan.

## Debt and Solvency Ratios

The next set of ratios to be considered are those related to the debt structure of an institution, and its ability to remain solvent, or to pay its bills as they come due. The first ratio, *debt-equity ratio*, provides a test of an institution's ability to access long-term credit and debt markets based on its current debt levels and expendable net assets (Fischer et al., 2004, p. 133; Prager, McCarthy, & Sealy, 2002, p. 23). The data for this calculation is typically found in the *statement of net assets* or the *statement of financial position*. Generally speaking, the *debt-equity ratio* takes the form:

Debt-equity Ratio = Expendable Net Assets/Long-Term Debt.

This happens where the numerator for the calculation comprises asset categories that include only the expendable, both restricted and unrestricted, portion of net assets. The denominator in this case "includes all notes, bonds, and capital leases payable" (Prager et al., 2002, p. 24) that fall under *noncurrent liabilities*. An overview of regularly included assets and debt types is provided in Table 4.3.

**Table 4.3   Regularly Included Asset and Debt Types**

| Expendable Net Assets | Long-Term Debt |
|---|---|
| Scholarships, research, instruction, other (R) | Capital leases |
| Loans (R) | Notes payable |
| Capital projects (R) | Bonds payable |
| Debt service (R) | Long-term debt payable |
| Unrestricted assets | |

(R) indicates that this asset is restricted but expendable.

When employing this measure of debt structure, there is no absolute "best" value. The measure instead can provide information regarding the sufficiency of expendable net assets to pay debt obligations as they come due. And while a ratio of 1:1 or higher suggests sufficient solvency, this may be too high or low based on institution-specific factors. Still, fiscal administrators should be wary of allowing this ratio to fall to far below the 1:1 ratio (Prager, McCarthy, & Sealy, 2002).

This is because a ratio that falls below the 1:1 threshold can signal to external stakeholders, including debt markets, that the institution is likely to have more difficulty being flexible and responding to adverse financial conditions. In other words, that the institution is likely suffering from internal resource limitations and is most liable to default in the future. However, the ratio only provides a quick glimpse of the viability of an institution based on its debt structure. As with other ratios, it should be one piece, not the only piece, of information and should be examined for trends over time.

The next two ratios that constitute a measure of an institution's debt structure and solvency include the *debt-service ratio*, which focuses on revenues (Chabotar, 1989, p. 196; Finkler et al., 2013, p. 574), and the *debt-service burden ratio*, which focuses on expenditures (Prager, McCarthy, & Sealy, 2002, p. 28). The debt-service ratio seeks to provide a quick metric of the relationship between current debt service and revenues and is calculated as:

Debt-Service Ratio = Debt-Service/Total Revenues.

Unlike the other primary debt structure ratio, the data required for these calculations include information from the *statement of cash flows*. Generally, included names and categories taken from the statement of cash flows under the heading *cash flows from capital financing and related activities* are

- principal payments on capital debt, including refunding activity;
- principal paid on capital leases; and
- interest paid on capital debt and leases.

Next, one is required to return to the statement of changes in revenues, expenditures, and net assets or statement of activities and obtain the value for total revenues, including nonoperating revenues for the denominator.

Similarly, the *debt-service burden ratio* seeks to understand the proportion of an institution's expenditures dedicated to servicing existing debt (Prager, McCarthy, & Sealy, 2002). This ratio employs the same numerator with the same information, but this time as a denominator, uses total expenditures as a comparison such that:

Debt-Service Burden Ratio = Debt-Service/Total Expenditures.

In this case, a hard-and-fast rule does not necessarily exist for nonprofits. Because higher education institutions can be both entities of the state, and private entities, it is difficult to provide definitive stance on an appropriate ratio here. Nonetheless, there exists some guidance. For example, Finkler et al. (2013, p. 575) and Chabotar (1989, p. 196) suggested that for the *debt-service ratio*, a good rule of thumb is 10% and surely less than 20% of operating revenues.

Arguably, the same rule of thumb holds for expenditures, though again, no real consensus exists around this number. And once more, it is necessary to stress that budget managers should be aware of the trend in these ratios. It is not enough to take a single cross-section and assume that this is a good indicator of the institution's debt-service or debt-service burden. Indeed, it is an analysis of the trend in either of these measures that signals whether an institution has leveraged itself appropriately and if it has sufficient flexibility to fund new capital projects while servicing previous ones.

## Source Ratios

While this section is called "source ratios," the reality is that a single calculation exists for determining the role played by a certain part of the revenue structure using information and data from the *statement of changes in revenues, expenses, and changes in net assets* or *statement of activities*. The *contribution ratio* is used to determine the proportion of a particular revenue component as compared to total expenditures such that (Chabotar, 1989, p. 197):

Contribution Ratio = Source of Revenue/Total Expenditures.

This allows the fiscal manager to determine the ratio, or percentage of revenues, from a single source compared to total expenditures. For example, assume that tuition and fee revenues are equal to $311,371 and that total expenditures are the same as before at $1,025,539. Then tuition and fees contribute just about 30.4% to expenditures. In other words, about one-third of expenditures rely on tuition and fees. As can be seen, this metric can provide useful information regarding the trends in revenue dependence to cover institutional operating expenses.

Additionally, the contribution ratio can provide a sense of how institutional revenue dependence tracks to expenses over time. This ratio can also show how changes in certain categories or sources have become more pronounced or have diminished as the external and internal environments respond to variability. While there exists little guidance around the proper ratios or pro-portions that institutions should maintain, at least a few things are true.

First, a goal should be to maintain revenue diversification so that changes in a single source do not have too severe an impact on overall institutional revenues or specific sources. Similar to investment portfolios, diversifying revenue reliance is sound fiscal practice.

Second, and related, should be maintaining flexibility. It becomes a prob-lem if flexibility is compromised and reliance upon a single or couple of revenue sources is high. Indeed, a major concern in determining creditworthi-ness and fiscal sustainability for higher education institutions is their ability to respond to a changing economic and political environment. Third, and finally, if reliance upon restricted revenue categories is increasing, this should be a cause for concern. This indicates that the institution has less control over resource allocation decisions.


## CAUTIONS ON FINANCIAL RATIO ANALYSIS

Before concluding this chapter, it is necessary to highlight a few cautions related to financial ratio analysis. First, a comprehensive decision-making process should employ financial ratios as well as financial report or state-ment notes and management's discussion to understand the institution's position more fully. Omitting this from the decision-making process, or from any process where the goal is to gain more far-reaching knowledge of fiscal administration, is folly.

Second, though it has been mentioned over and over again in this chap-ter, the use of multiple years of data and trend analysis is crucial in applied budgeting and fiscal administration of colleges and universities. Moreover, using multiple years of data and trends can help guide decision-makers to make clearer connections between financial ratio analysis and strategic plans and goals.

Third, it is almost never the case that a single ratio can provide sufficient information. Using multiple ratios over many years can help to alleviate some of the obscuring effects of using only one. Additionally, using multiple points of data, information, and metrics provides a solid foundation for decision-making that is interested in maintaining fiscal sustainability.

Fourth, when calculating ratios, make certain that the ownership and issu-ance of debt and assets by university foundations, auxiliary enterprises, and other financially related entities are presented. If this is not done, significant questions may arise, and it is unethical not to present the full financial picture or circumstances facing the institution. This is especially important for the calculation of debt-equity or debt-service ratios.

For example, if debt is issued or refinanced by either the institution or related entity, the fiscal manager should look to the included financial statement notes and instead employ the contractual principal amount rather than the amount reported in the statement of cash flows (Prager, McCarthy, & Sealy, 2002, p. 29). Finally, the overarching principle for ratio analysis should be to examine this information over time so that a single difficult or anomalous year does not lead to bad decision-making.

## CONCLUSION

The goal of this chapter has been to provide new fiscal managers, budgeters, and decision-makers with financial responsibilities in colleges and universities, with some basic information around financial ratios and their analysis. Ideally, the content of this chapter has provided a foundational understanding of the primary elements and uses of financial ratio in the fiscal administration of colleges and universities. The discussion in this chapter has limited itself to only those ratios that would likely hold the most relevance in the day-to-day operations of an institution. In addition, the discussion has sought not only to present the ratios themselves, but to indicate where the data and information "live," in an effort to demystify the process to some extent. It has also provided a quick guide to some of the pitfalls and limitations presented by financial ratio analysis. By presenting financial ratio analysis in this manner, this chapter sets a foundation for the rest of the text's material and exercises.

## QUESTIONS AND EXERCISES ON RATIO ANALYSIS IN HIGHER EDUCATION

1. Why do higher education administrators and analysts use ratios? What are some of the best uses of ratio analysis?
2. Explain some of the major differences between public and private ratio analysis.
3. What are some cautions that fiscal managers should consider when using ratio analysis? How does this relate to human judgment in the process?
4. Which types of ratios (categories) are typically useful to higher education institutions?
5. How should a fiscal manager treat foundation or endowment monies, liabilities, and other financial matters in ratio analysis?
6. Using the financial statements included in Figure 4.6, please calculate the following liquidity ratios using Table 4.1 and its categories for your calculations:

**ASSETS**
**Current assets**

| | | |
|---|---|---|
| Cash and cash equivalents | $ 574,506 | $ 383,786 |
| Accounts receivable, net | 114,030 | 130,870 |
| Current portion of notes and pledges receivable | 11,086 | 10,881 |
| Inventories | 9,501 | 15,659 |
| Short-term investments | 20,351 | 20,506 |
| Securities lending assets | 77,920 | 97,985 |
| Other assets | 21,739 | 20,935 |
| Total current assets | 829,133 | 680,622 |

**Noncurrent assets**

| | | |
|---|---|---|
| Accounts receivable | 15,303 | 2,426 |
| Notes and pledges receivable | 75,406 | 71,515 |
| Investments | 715,369 | 778,704 |
| Capital assets, net | 2,048,204 | 1,933,451 |
| Total noncurrent assets | 2,854,282 | 2,786,096 |
| **Total assets** | **3,683,415** | **3,466,718** |

**LIABILITIES**
**Current liabilities**

| | | |
|---|---|---|
| Accounts payable and accrued liabilities | 210,039 | 197,143 |
| Deferred revenue | 138,069 | 147,391 |
| Current portion of capital lease obligations | 1,518 | 1,570 |
| Current portion of long-term debt | 51,312 | 41,067 |
| Securities lending liabilities | 77,920 | 97,985 |
| Total current liabilities | 478,858 | 485,156 |

**Noncurrent liabilities**

| | | |
|---|---|---|
| Capital lease obligations | 9,064 | 9,942 |
| Notes payable | 4,101 | 141,290 |
| Assets held in custody for others | 66,577 | 65,923 |
| Deferred revenue | 48,729 | 24,778 |
| Bonds payable | 725,723 | 534,898 |
| Other long-term liabilities | 18,399 | 12,103 |
| Total noncurrent liabilities | 872,593 | 788,934 |
| **Total liabilities** | **1,351,451** | **1,274,090** |

**NET ASSETS**

| | | |
|---|---|---|
| Invested in capital assets, net of related debt | 1,336,766 | 1,304,656 |
| Restricted for: | | |
|   Nonexpendable - endowments | 67,508 | 73,025 |
|   Expendable | | |
|     Scholarships, research, instruction and other | 85,480 | 91,866 |
|     Loans | 23,182 | 22,357 |
|     Capital projects | 14,122 | 13,247 |
|     Debt service | 21,536 | 23,482 |
| Unrestricted | 783,370 | 663,995 |
| **Total net assets** | **2,331,964** | **2,192,628** |
| **Total liabilities and net assets** | **$3,683,415** | **$3,466,718** |

Figure 4.6  *Statement of Net Assets* for Chapter Exercises. *Source*: Edited by Authors, Public Records: Multiple Institutions.

| | | |
|---|---|---|
| **OPERATING REVENUES** | | |
| Student fees | $ 878,229 | $ 785,127 |
| Less scholarship allowance | (114,154) | (98,006) |
| Federal grants and contracts | 290,929 | 286,687 |
| State and local grants and contracts | 21,100 | 25,153 |
| Nongovernmental grants and contracts | 107,146 | 121,853 |
| Sales and services of educational units | 48,929 | 49,108 |
| Other revenue | 171,284 | 185,891 |
| Auxiliary enterprises (net of scholarship allowance of $13,796 in 2008 and $12,245 in 2007) | 319,153 | 336,397 |
| **Total operating revenues** | 1,722,616 | 1,692,210 |
| **OPERATING EXPENSES** | | |
| Compensation and benefits | 1,535,335 | 1,455,868 |
| Student financial aid | 109,566 | 98,061 |
| Energy and utilities | 57,773 | 52,409 |
| Travel | 39,481 | 36,231 |
| Supplies and general expense | 428,521 | 469,503 |
| Depreciation and amortization expense | 116,683 | 111,860 |
| **Total operating expenses** | 2,287,359 | 2,223,932 |
| **Total operating loss** | (564,743) | (531,722) |
| **NONOPERATING REVENUES (EXPENSES)** | | |
| State appropriations | 558,022 | 527,747 |
| Grants and contracts | 51,317 | 46,285 |
| Investment income | 30,721 | 85,462 |
| Gifts | 77,272 | 67,398 |
| Interest expense | (36,335) | (35,952) |
| **Net nonoperating revenues** | 680,997 | 690,940 |
| **Income before other revenues, expenses, gains, or losses** | 116,254 | 159,218 |
| Capital appropriations | 12,601 | 10,467 |
| Capital gifts and grants | 10,217 | 3,311 |
| Additions to permanent endowments | 264 | 2,147 |
| **Total other revenues** | 23,082 | 15,925 |
| **Increase in net assets** | 139,336 | 175,143 |
| **Net assets, beginning of year** | 2,192,628 | 2,017,485 |
| **Net assets, end of year** | $2,331,964 | $2,192,628 |

**Figure 4.7** *Statement of Revenues, Expenses, and Changes in Net Assets* for Chapter Exercises. *Source*: Edited by Authors, Public Records: Multiple Institutions.

    a. Current ratio
    b. Quick ratio
    c. Available funds ratio
    d. Briefly describe how each of these differs from one another.
7. Using the financial statements included in Figure 4.7, please calculate the following operating performance ratios using Table 4.2 and its categories for your calculations:

| **CASH FLOWS FROM OPERATING ACTIVITIES** | | |
|---|---:|---:|
| Student fees | $ 766,000 | $ 693,977 |
| Grants and contracts | 405,897 | 389,542 |
| Sales and services of educational activities | 47,988 | 63,634 |
| Auxiliary enterprise charges | 315,580 | 336,318 |
| Other operating receipts | 165,802 | 166,716 |
| Payments to employees | (1,526,190) | (1,427,753) |
| Payments to suppliers | (485,354) | (552,234) |
| Student financial aid | (112,375) | (98,850) |
| Student loans collected | 9,411 | 12,376 |
| Student loans issued | (14,613) | (15,630) |
| Net cash used in operating activities | (427,854) | (431,904) |
| **CASH FLOWS FROM NONCAPITAL FINANCING ACTIVITIES** | | |
| State appropriations | 570,194 | 543,414 |
| Nonoperating grants and contracts | 52,356 | 46,285 |
| Gifts and grants received for other than capital purposes | 77,206 | 71,362 |
| Direct lending receipts | 440,162 | 413,093 |
| Direct lending payments | (440,948) | (412,808) |
| Net cash provided by noncapital financing activities | 698,970 | 661,346 |
| **CASH FLOWS FROM CAPITAL AND RELATED FINANCING ACTIVITIES** | | |
| Capital appropriations | 12,601 | 10,467 |
| Capital grants and gifts received | 47,340 | 2,208 |
| Purchase of capital assets | (261,030) | (216,797) |
| Proceeds from issuance of capital debt, including refunding activity | 289,754 | 85,000 |
| Principal payments on capital debt, including refunding activity | (224,948) | (39,219) |
| Principal paid on capital leases | (1,760) | (2,158) |
| Interest paid on capital debt and leases | (36,249) | (33,823) |
| Net cash used in capital and related financing activities | (174,292) | (194,322) |
| **CASH FLOWS FROM INVESTING ACTIVITIES** | | |
| Proceeds from sales and maturities of investments | 2,239,333 | 1,805,801 |
| Investment income | 40,658 | 59,402 |
| Purchase of investments | (2,186,095) | (1,993,213) |
| Net cash provided (used) by investing activities | 93,896 | (128,010) |
| Net increase (decrease) in cash and cash equivalents | 190,720 | (92,890) |
| Cash and cash equivalents, beginning of year | 383,786 | 476,676 |
| Cash and cash equivalents, end of year | $ 574,506 | $ 383,786 |

Figure 4.8a    *Statement of Cash Flows* for Chapter Exercises. *Source*: Edited by Authors, Public Records: Multiple Institutions.

   a. Net operating ratio
   b. Program/function ratio for student aid expenditures
   c. Revised net operating ratio
   d. Briefly discuss why the net operating ratio and revised net operating ratio would differ for a public college or university.
8. Using the financial statements included in Figures 4.8a and 4.8b, please calculate the following debt and solvency ratios using Table 4.3 and its categories for your calculations:
   a. Debt-equity ratio
   b. Debt-service ratio
   c. Debt-service burden ratio
   d. Briefly discuss what each of these ratios is measuring and how they differ.

RECONCILIATION OF OPERATING LOSS TO NET CASH USED IN OPERATING ACTIVITIES:
*(in thousands of dollars)*

| | Fiscal Year Ended | |
| | June 30, 2008 | June 30, 2007 |
|---|---|---|
| Operating loss | $ (564,743) | $ (531,722) |
| Adjustments to reconcile operating loss to net cash used in operating activities: | | |
| Depreciation and amortization expense | 116,683 | 111,860 |
| Loss on disposal of capital assets | 22,246 | 15,053 |
| Changes in assets and liabilities: | | |
| Accounts receivable | 6,450 | (4,583) |
| Inventories | 6,158 | 1,410 |
| Other assets | (804) | (7,042) |
| Notes receivable | (3,311) | (2,706) |
| Accounts payable and accrued liabilities | 11,887 | 24,912 |
| Deferred revenue | (29,370) | (39,789) |
| Assets held in custody for others | 654 | (276) |
| Other noncurrent liabilities | 6,296 | 979 |
| Net cash used in operating activities | $ (427,854) | $ (431,904) |

*See accompanying notes to the financial statements.*

**Figure 4.8b** *(Continued).*

9. Using the financial statements included, please calculate the source ratios for each of the following contribution areas:
   a. Tuition and fees
   b. State appropriations (nonoperating revenue)
   c. Federal grants and contracts
   d. Other revenues
   e. What do these contribution ratios suggest about the institution's reliance on certain revenues?

## NOTES

1. These example documents were reproduced with permission from each university's finance or treasury office.

2. The "financing" in the statement of cash flows includes revenues and expenditures that impacted cash flows not directly derived from operations. For public higher education, a major category is often "state appropriations."

3. The use of unrestricted or total revenues is likely to be a local decision and will depend on the goal of estimate conservativeness.

4. Though considered nonoperating revenue (revenue not derived directly from operations), these revenues, nonetheless, make up a portion of the operating budget. In other words, they are generally unrestricted revenues and are usable for the general operation of the institution.

# Chapter 5

# Forecasting, Accuracy, and Judgment

Forecasting is the practice of making predictions about a future state of affairs (Dunn, 2012; Stevenson, 2015). While there are many techniques for doing so, the basics of accurate forecasting require at least three factors: good data, good local contextual knowledge, and good analysts.[1] First, the importance of good data should be self-evident to those with budgeting responsibilities. Good data provide the backbone for accurate forecasting, which assists in decision-making at all levels. Without good data, forecasts are unreliable.

Therefore, analysts should know their data well. Second, budgeters are often required to make predictions about the financial standing of the organization as well as to anticipate what might occur based on knowledge of the past. This type of contextual information tends not to be taught in a classroom but rather is specific to the local conditions and organizational culture.

In order for forecasting to be accurate and for budgeters to provide useful information, a solid understanding of the context is vital. The final piece of accurate forecasting is good analysts. Accurate and useful forecasting requires a certain set of technical and analytical know-how. The goal of this chapter is to provide the reader with the necessary know-how to accurately forecast.

This chapter presents forecasting foundations. After reading this chapter, students should be prepared to carry out basic forecasting techniques. They will also be exposed to the multiple techniques available to them, including linear, nonlinear, and expert judgment approaches. Moreover, students will examine some of the limitations of forecasting and appropriate expectations around the uses of forecasting results. It is important to note that the techniques presented in this chapter extend well beyond the anticipation of enrollments to costs and revenues as well. In fact, many of the techniques offered here can be used to anticipate many possible fiscal states of affairs in just about any educational context.

## EXPECTATIONS AND USES OF FORECASTING RESULTS

For the most part forecasting should be seen as one more piece of information for decision-making. Forecasting can provide decision-makers with "what if" analyses that vary conditions in multiple scenarios (Rylee, 2011) and that might include conditions under which the status quo is assumed. In doing so, the forecast can help decision-makers consider the consequences of multiple courses of action. It can also help buffer the institution against threats and opportunities that arise. However, forecasting should not be seen as the single or even the best way to make decisions.

Forecasting should be one piece of information that takes into account possible scenarios or future states of affairs that incorporates local knowledge and analytical expertise. While forecasts can serve as a basis for decision-making, good forecasts include two important caveats. First, all forecasts will be off by some amount. The goal of forecasting is to get as close as possible to the true value based on good data, good local knowledge, and good technical expertise. When forecasts deviate a great deal from the actual value, it may be necessary to examine these variances and review the underlying assumptions going into the forecasting approach. Techniques for conducting variance analysis are covered in chapter 7 of this text.

Second, all forecasts are subject to sudden and unexpected deviations based on unanticipated events. For example, the economic reverberations from the bursting of the housing bubble in 2008 created difficulties for local and state governments, which in turn impacted educational appropriations and support. It is unlikely that this type of fluctuation would have been accounted for by forecasting models employing historical data, though some might argue that local knowledge and technical expertise should have accounted for this to some extent. Nonetheless, it is always important to note that these types of events result in massive variances between the forecasted and actual values even if the best data, analysts, and techniques are employed.

## FORECASTING APPROACHES AND METHODS

Generally speaking, there are three categories of forecasting approaches: averages, linear, and curvilinear. This section will highlight the uses, advantages, and limitations of each. It also provides a foray into the actual techniques themselves and a hypothetical dataset for practice problems at the end of this chapter. It is important to highlight that the use of forecasting techniques assumes that time-series data (data for multiple years, months, days, etc.) are available. It is the nature of time-series data that allows one to extrapolate from past events to possible future ones (Dunn, 2012). Let us now turn to the first approach—forecasting by averages.

## Using Averages for Forecasting

This type of forecasting typically employs averages of historical data to predict future values. The benefit of using this type of forecasting technique is based upon its dependence on historical information. The inclusion of data that fluctuate upward and downward means that the use of averages smooths variability. It is also advantageous to use this method because averages tend to reflect the random variation of data. This means that the information provided by this technique can allow decision-makers to react to needed changes rather than simply minor variations (Finkler et al., 2013; Stevenson, 2015). In other words, small variations based on smoothing provided by averages indicate that budget analysts and managers should focus on large deviations and what these could mean for decision-making.

While this technique readily lends itself to practical use because of its ease of both formulation and interpretation, some important limitations exist. First, the use of historical data and the "moving" part of the average shows that this technique can be very sensitive to the number of data points included.[2] This is because when the moving average calculates each new forecast point, it picks up the next period's data point and drops the last period. This also means that each value is given equal weight.

Second, depending on how many points are included from the most recent or furthest away period, the forecasted value can vary considerably (Stevenson, 2015). In other words, if more data points are included from time periods further away from the present, the smoothing effect of past events becomes more pronounced. If a greater number of points are included from more recent periods, then the forecast will weight recent events more heavily. The point here is that budget managers should be aware of the tradeoffs made when certain data or assumptions guide the forecast.

To make this more concrete, let's look at a fictional dataset that is used for the rest of the chapter, and compare how different choices around data inclusion change forecasts. It is necessary to highlight that here the analysis uses forecasting for calculating future student enrollments; however, all of the techniques presented here are fully applicable to revenues and expenditures. Indeed, to obtain a revenue estimate, one simply needs to use the methods outlined here and multiple forecasted revenue or expenditures by forecasted student numbers.

**Table 5.1  Fictional Dataset for Forecasting Student Enrollments**

| Time/Period | # of Students | Weights for Three-Period | Weights for Five-Period |
|---|---|---|---|
| 1 | 15,123 | | |
| 2 | 16,345 | | |
| 3 | 17,567 | | |
| 4 | 18,789 | | |
| 5 | 19,901 | | |
| 6 | 20,123 | | .10 |
| 7 | 21,456 | | .15 |
| 8 | 22,000 | .15 | .20 |
| 9 | 23,678 | .35 | .25 |
| 10 | 24,922 | .50 | .30 |
| | Total Weight | 1.0 | 1.0 |

Using the data in Table 5.1, we calculate a three-period *basic moving average* and a five-period basic moving average for forecasting the expected number of students for period 11. We will also move from the more basic moving average forecasting technique to weighted moving average and use some examples that compare the two techniques.

To carry out this calculation we will need a few pieces of information. Using Stevenson's (2015, p. 86) example, the following equation provides a basic framework for calculating a moving average:

$$Forecast_t = Moving\ Average_n = \frac{\sum_{i=1}^{n} A_i}{n}.$$

This happens when the forecast for the time period under consideration is equal to the moving average of a certain number of periods. The moving average is calculated by taking each value for the periods to be included (for our first example, the last three periods) and summing them together. Then this value is divided by the total of time points included. This equation would indicate that the following equation for our dataset is correct:

$$F_{11} = MA_{3-period} = \frac{22,000 + 23,678 + 24,922}{3} = 23,533.3.$$

Hence, our forecasted number of students for time period 11 based on a three-period moving average is 23,533.3. Now let's consider a five-period moving average example using the same data.

$$F_{11} = MA_{5-period} = \frac{20,123 + 21,456 + 22,000 + 23,678 + 24,922}{5} = 22,435.8.$$

As can be seen, the forecasted number of students based on a three-period average instead of a five-period one results in a difference of forecasted students of 1,097.5. This difference in estimates using just two more years of data shows two things. First, the inclusion of more data has impacted the forecast by what might be considered a large amount. This basic example should show how sensitive estimates are to the number of data points used as well as how distance from the present affects the forecast. In other words, this is why moving averages typically do not employ a ten or twenty period.

Second, local context about environmental factors and budget management/philosophy will often dictate how many years of data will be appropriate for use. It is therefore imperative that the assumptions going into the forecasting model and technique itself are understood clearly (Dunn, 2012).

Turning to *weighted moving average*, the basic premise is the same as the more basic technique with one exception—weights are assigned to time periods to indicate relative importance of some over others instead of simply dividing by the total number of included years. The advantage of this more advanced technique is that it assigns heavier weight to recent events that might impact the estimated value of some important variable. We should underscore that the weights used over the time period must sum to one (Stevenson, 2015). Using a similar equation as earlier, the weighted moving average calculation includes these weights as follows for three periods:

$$F_{11} = WMA_{3-period} = .15(22,000) + .35(23,678) + .50(24,922) = 24,048.3.$$

Doing the same for five periods the equation is:

$$F_{11} = WMA_{5-period}$$
$$= .10(20,123) + .15(21,456) + .20(22,000) + .25(23,678) + .30(24,922)$$
$$= 23,026.8.$$

Once again, what becomes evident is that the method and assumptions that go into the forecasting approach and methodology employed impact our estimates. In the weighted example, the difference in the three- and five-period estimates still sits at over 1,000 (1,021.5 to be exact). As stated earlier, a benefit of this technique is that it explicitly sets weights to time periods so as to account for the relative importance of more recent events as compared with earlier ones while still including information from dates that are further away from the present.

A primary limitation of this approach is that the choice of weights for each period of data included is rather subjective and may require multiple iterations to determine the appropriate weighting format (Stevenson, 2015).

In other words, local context and human judgment will drive the choice of weight rather than some external process.

This brief section has outlined two techniques for using moving averages to forecast future values. While we have provided two examples using three- and five-period averages, budgeters should note that the number of years used in this type of forecasting approach is reliant upon what is considered appropriate based on context, local information, and data availability.

It is also important to highlight that forecasts can be extended for many time periods beyond the available data using the calculated averages as done earlier, for future periods with the same caveats presented before. Also, in the process of forecasting, data variations based upon seasonality, secular trends, and business cycles should be taken into account. That is, when variations are examined, large deviations from averages might be due to external, but well-known, factors such as those just noted (Dunn, 2012; Finkler et al., 2013).

## Exponential Smoothing

As just noted, weighted averages allow for budget managers to explicitly assign importance to certain time periods when making forecasts. In *exponential smoothing*, a similar weighting occurs, but in this case the forecast is dependent upon the value of the previous period's forecast and a percentage of the forecasting error (Stevenson, 2015). In other words, rather than assign an explicit weight to each time period, this method smooths the next estimate by evenly spreading the weight using a constant percentage of the forecasting error from one time period to the next. Because this method is closely related to understanding forecasting accuracy, in this section we introduce only the basic mechanics behind the technique.

Generally speaking, the next forecast's value $(F_t)$ is equal to the sum of the previous forecast's value $(F_{t-1})$ and the product of the forecasting error $(A_{t-1} - F_{t-1})$, where the actual and previous forecasts are subtracted from one another, and the smoothing constant $(\alpha)$, which is equal to a percentage of the forecasting error. To make this more concrete, Stevenson (2015, p. 89) provides the following formula:

$$F_t = F_{t-1} + \propto \left( A_{t-1} - F_{t-1} \right).$$

This formula readily lends itself to straightforward implementation. To illustrate, let's use information from the dataset presented earlier. Assume that the goal is to estimate the next time period's enrollment values and that thus far we have employed a three-period moving average technique to do so. Since we have already calculated the moving average using the last three periods of data, which is often recommended (Stevenson, 2015, p. 5), we can now quickly calculate the forecasted enrollments for period 12 ($F_{12}$) using exponential smoothing. First, assume that the forecasted value,[3] 23,533.3 for period 11, was off by 500 students so that the actual value equals approximately 23,033 for ease of analysis.

Second, assume that the smoothing constant ($\alpha$) is .15. With this information, the next step is to correctly specify the values for each part of the equation. The equation for this example should look like this:

$$F_{12} = 23,533.3 + .15(23,033.3 - 23,533.3) = 23,458.3.$$

This estimate directly accounts for the error between forecasted and actual values when projecting the next time period's forecast. If one wishes to use exponential smoothing for the next period ($F_{13}$), then the method is the same. To demonstrate, assume that the actual demand for period 12 ($F_{12}$) is off by 250 students so that the actual number is 23,208.3. Then, the equation for period 13 takes the following form:

$$F_{13} = 23,458.3 + .15(23,208.3 - 23,458.3) = 23,420.8.$$

Based upon the assumptions regarding the smoothing constant, the budget manager can continue to project future values in this way.

While a more powerful and sophisticated tool than averaging methods, there are some important limitations to employing this technique. Much like the weighted moving average presented earlier, exponential smoothing requires rather subjective decisions regarding the smoothing constant. In most instances, the smoothing constant takes on a value of between .05 and .50, where lower values assume stability in the underlying averages and higher numbers just the opposite (Stevenson, 2015).

Additionally, the forecasted values become more reactive and less smooth as the value of the smoothing constant increases from zero to one. This means that the budget manager should have a valid and clear rationale for the choice of a smoothing constant level even when using software that can automatically change $\alpha$ values when errors become too large.

## Correlation Analysis

Before moving to the more sophisticated analysis of two variables, it is important to highlight a relatively easy and extremely useful measure for forecasting relationships among two variables-correlation analysis. While the previous section has provided a clear approach for forecasting using averages, this technique is focused more so upon the movement of variables in relation to one another over time.

The usefulness of correlation analysis instead of, or with, regression analysis is that it provides a readily accessible measure of the magnitude of relationship between two variables over an certain period of time. Say, for example, that we wish to examine the relationship between tuition and fee levels and state support to a college or university for the past ten years.

The measure of correlation (Pearson $r$) can tell us how strong this relationship is and can easily be carried out for a number of variables simultaneously with Excel or other statistical software packages. The general equation[4] for computing this relationship is as follows (Stevenson, 2015, p. 104):

$$r = \frac{n\left(\sum xy\right) - \left(\sum x\right)\left(\sum y\right)}{\sqrt{n\left(\sum x^2\right) - \left(\sum x\right)^2} \sqrt{n\left(\sum y^2\right) - \left(\sum y\right)^2}}.$$

As the measure is bounded between 1 and +1, it can tell us both the direction and strength of the relationship. For the most part, relationships ranging from .70 to .80 and above are considered strong, between .30 and .70 moderate, and below .30 weak (Stevenson, 2015; Trochim & Donnelly, 2007). Additionally, the sign indicates the direction of the relationship. So, for example, let's say that tuition and state support share a .85 relationship.

This would suggest that tuition and state support move in a strong and opposite direction from one another. If the negative sign were left off, then it would be clear that the two would share a strong positive relationship indicating that they move in a similar direction (if one moves up the other tends to as well and vice versa). When used appropriately, budget managers can forecast expected relationships and their magnitude to determine, roughly, the expected or forecasted impact of a certain course of events or decisions.

When coupled with regression analysis, this makes for an especially powerful prediction tool. What is more, many statistical software packages and Excel include a canned option for determining if the relationship is statistically significant.[5]

Finally, when used with regression analysis, the square of the correlation coefficient ($r$) provides an easily understandable measure for estimating how much of the variance in the dependent variable is explained by the independent variable or variables (if used with multiple regression). The interpretation of the $r^2$ coefficient is similar to that of the interpretation of the $r$-coefficient earlier. However, in this instance, the $r^2$ statistic is telling us how well the independent variable ($x$) accounts for the variance in the dependent variable ($y$).

Another caveat is that this goodness-of-fit statistic is always positive given that it is the square of the correlation coefficient. Readers should note that the $r^2$ statistic is only one of a variety of goodness-of-fit measures. For example, a typical goodness-of-fit measure for categorical data is a chi-square ($\chi^2$)

statistic. Hence, it is imperative that the budget manager understand the data and how best to use different forecasting techniques and tools for making appropriate budget projections.

## Using Linear Models and Regression for Forecasting

Linear models and regression analysis provide a good predictive approach to forecasting based upon linear trends rather than averages. In its most basic form a linear model is expressed as:

$$Y_t = a + b(x).$$

In this case, $Y_t$ is equal to our forecasted value in time $t$; $a$ is equal to our intercept which is the value that $Y_t$ would take on if $x$ equals zero; $b$ is equal to the slope of the line of best fit; and, $x$ is our independent variable. Essentially, this model is telling us that $Y$ (our forecasted value for time $t$) will be equal to the sum of the baseline intercept ($a$) and $x$ multiplied by $b$.

For many individuals who have not had statistics in some time, or who are unfamiliar with this equation at all, $b$ in the equation is simply telling us how $Y_t$ changes when $x$ changes. Based on the purposes of this chapter, $x$ will be equal to our time period $t$. So our equation looks exactly the same as before but with $t$ standing in for $x$ (Stevenson, 2015). This formula allows us to calculate trend values when we assume that the relationship between $x$ and $y$ is linear. This model expresses the relationship between $x$ and $y$ formally, and also makes assumptions about this relationship as just noted (Dunn, 2012).

## Regression Forecasting

Before moving to the specific mechanics of regression forecasting, we should underscore the important distinctions regarding correlational and causal analysis. Many individuals who employ regression techniques for forecasting are often unaware of these distinctions. As each type of analysis introduces certain assumptions, only fundamental differences are explored.

First, and in most instances, budgeters will carry out correlational forecasting. This means that the relationships examined and explained using regression analysis should be understood in terms of their association, *not causes*. That is, interpretation of the estimates of the relationship between $x$ and $y$ should be expressed as associations (they move in relation to one another in such and such a manner) and not that $x$ causes $y$.

If one wishes to make causal claims, there are techniques for doing so. Causal analysis makes claims regarding the impact of $x$ on $y$ in terms of cause and effect; $x$ causes $y$ and is not simply associated with it. While this is an important distinction, it is outside the scope of the current text to explore causal analysis as a topic because it requires much more sophisticated estimation techniques.[6]

Additionally, it is possible to employ multiple regression when more than one explanatory variable (*x*) is used for forecasting. This technique allows for the inclusion of many known drivers of specific outcome variable (*y*). For those interested in a detailed treatment of these two subjects, we suggest referencing Box & Jenkins (2008) and Stevenson (2015).

Returning to linear regression, the most typical modeling choice used by budgeters is ordinary least squares (OLS). This seeks to find a straight line that minimizes the distance of the historical data points from the line of best fit. For example, in Figure 5.1, all ten data points for the number of students are plotted (squares) and a line (linear trend) is fitted.

A much-touted benefit of using regression analysis in forecasting is that its assumptions are clear, and it is relatively easy to implement using Excel or statistical packages such as SPSS, STATA, or SAS. Additionally, the linear trend line calculated using OLS is as close as possible to the historical data points. As noted by Finkler et al. (2013), not only is it unlikely that all historical points would fall along a straight line, but any other line would be further away as well. This means that the closeness of the line to historical data points will result in future estimated points that are closer to the actual future values.

Let's look at an example using our fictional dataset from Table 5.2. First, one should plot the data to determine whether or not a linear trend is evident.

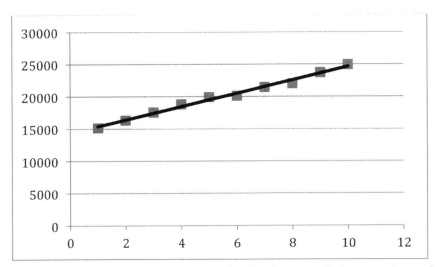

**Figure 5.1  Example of Data Points Plotted with Linear Trend Line Superimposed.**
*Source*: Authors.

From Figure 5.1, we can see that it is. Now recall that our model takes the form:

$$Y_t = a + b(t).$$

So in order to employ this model correctly, we must find the values of $a$ and $b$ that will provide us with a linear trend based on the assumptions of OLS. To do so we need two more equations. To calculate our $b$ value, we will need to use the formula that follows. Following Stevenson (2015, p. 93), this is expressed formally as:

$$b = \frac{n \sum tY - \sum t \sum y}{n \sum (t^2) - \left( \sum t \right)^2}.$$

Therefore, for our example, it should be:

$$b = \frac{10(1,184,427) - 55(199,904)}{10(385) - 55(55)} \text{ or } 1,029.76.$$

Readers should notice that the value of $\Sigma tY$ (1,184,427) is different than the value of $\Sigma t \Sigma y$ (10,994,720); this matters computationally for the estimating equation. For our next variable the formal expression is:

$$a = \frac{\sum Y - b \sum t}{n}.$$

Therefore, for our example here, the values should be:

$$a = \frac{199,904 - 1,029.76(55)}{10} \text{ or } 14,326.72.$$

Based on this information, the linear trend line is equal to:

$$Y_t = 14,326.72 + 1,029.76(t).$$

Therefore, if we wish to estimate what the forecasted number of students will be based on OLS estimates, we simply plug that number in for $t$. In this case, we would expect that student numbers would be equal to 25,654.08 (14,326.72 + 1,029.76(11)). Say that we wish to do the same thing for period 13. We simply employ the same technique and come up with 27,713.60 (14,326.72 + 1,029.76(13)).

As is evident, the linear models employed here return much higher forecasts on student numbers than any of the averaging techniques. This short

**Table 5.2   Fictional Dataset for Forecasting Student Enrollments Using Linear Regression (OLS)**

| Time/Period (t) | Number of Students (Y) | Time* Number of Students (t * y) | Time-Squared ($t^2$) |
|---|---|---|---|
| 1 | 15,123 | 15,123 | 1 |
| 2 | 16,345 | 32,690 | 4 |
| 3 | 17,567 | 52,701 | 9 |
| 4 | 18,789 | 75,156 | 16 |
| 5 | 19,901 | 99,505 | 25 |
| 6 | 20,123 | 120,738 | 36 |
| 7 | 21,456 | 150,192 | 49 |
| 8 | 22,000 | 176,000 | 64 |
| 9 | 23,678 | 213,102 | 81 |
| 10 | 24,922 | 249,220 | 100 |
| $\Sigma_t = 55$ | $\Sigma_y = 199,904$ | $\Sigma_{ty} = 1,184,427$ | $t^2 = 385$ |

illustration should serve as a good example of the ways in which the underlying structure and specific approaches impact the resulting forecast.

While regression analysis is a powerful tool for forecasting, some limitations remain. First, we must make sure that the relationship being modeled makes sense. If not, estimates will not be valid. Next, just like any forecasting technique, the assumptions about the data can limit the usefulness of the results. If inappropriate assumptions have been made, the analysis is for naught.

Another consideration is that simple regression analysis is only appropriate for the case where there is one dependent ($Y$) variable and one independent ($X$) variable. If not, then other techniques that include multivariate regression should be considered. Also, the data requirements for regression analysis tend to be rather large with the minimum number of observations being 20–30 for valid forecasting (Stevenson, 2015).

Finally, the linear technique presented here makes a very strong statement about the relationship of the variables. If the data do not share a linear relationship, the use of this technique is not correct (Finkler et al., 2013). Techniques for dealing with this situation are presented in the next section on curvilinear models.

## CURVILINEAR MODELS: A BRIEF OVERVIEW

The previous section highlighted the benefits and limitations of regression analysis and linear assumptions. While it is clear that regression analysis is a powerful tool in the forecaster's arsenal, a major limitation remains. Namely, that the linear approach is based on the assumption that the relationships under examination follow a straight line (Finkler et al., 2013) as graphed in Figure 5.1. When relationships among variables do not exist in this manner, there are ways to either deal with the curvilinear nature of the relationship or employ mathematical transformations of the data to make it more linear.

Typically, forecasters will encounter four types of curvilinear trends in a set of data: exponential, logarithmic, polynomial, and power. While we treat moving averages as its own approach in this chapter, it should be understood that moving averages can also have curvilinear traits and, therefore, data should be plotted, if possible, before imposing a trend line upon it.

First is exponential transformation of the data. What this does is to transform the data into an exponential function that can show underlying trends based on a value changing in an increasingly upward or downward manner. Next is the logarithmic transformation approach. This transformation method is especially good for data that exhibits rapid changes that smooth out over time or that clearly shows growth or decline that is persistent. This is an approach that is often used to help smooth data fluctuations that, if graphed or examined in their raw state, would make interpretation difficult.

Another approach is the polynomial (cyclical) method, which is especially useful for data that varies in a cyclical fashion (up and down) over time. The reason for such variability is often due to timing, seasonality, or economic cycles. Finally, power trends are useful for data that displays a relationship where the values of the data are increasing at a specific rate at regular points

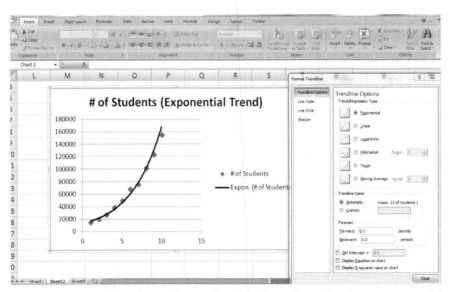

**Figure 5.2 Screenshot of Trendline Options in Microsoft Excel Using an Exponential Trend.** *Source*: Authors.

over time. A limitation of this approach, however, is that because it employs a power equation, it cannot deal with values that are either zero or negative (Dunn, 2012; Finkler et al., 2013; Stevenson, 2015).

The great thing about using any type of trend line is that there exist many software packages that either specialize in this, or that can provide tools for carrying out a trend analysis. For example, Excel provides a great and readily accessible means for plotting data and examining trends. Figure 5.2 illustrates the available trend line options.[7]

## JUDGMENT IN FORECASTING

For much of this chapter the focus has been on rather mechanistic methods of forecasting future states of events. In this section, we turn to what is arguably the most important component of good forecasting—human judgment. As noted throughout this chapter, the assumptions made about the data, relationships, and local variables, which are all based on human judgment, underpin the relevance and utility of forecasts. To help explain this role more carefully, we will consider the function of multiple factors that impact the forecasting process in turn.

The budget manager plays a direct role in the forecasting of future events/ values that matter to decision-making. In many cases, it is the budget manager's role to determine which assumptions should be included in the model. In some cases, the manager chooses the approach. In any event, the budget manager can have a great deal of influence over forecasts as well as their validity when choices are based on the information available. For example, a fluctuation in an external variable may be of great consequence to one individual when conducting a forecast and of little importance to another.

Another important and related consideration is the role of budget philosophy. As highlighted in chapter 1, because educational organizations tend to have processes in place for allocating resources, knowing how this might impact the forecasting approach and assumptions is very important. Regardless of the type of approach employed locally, most managers develop a forecasting style that mirrors their philosophy of budget management.

However, even the best educational leaders should take care not to remain too committed to a budgeting philosophy that may or may not reflect the current and anticipated circumstances facing the organization. Instead, historical data, sound analysis, and scanning of the external environment for possible instability can contribute to an optimal forecasting strategy.

Finally, the role of expertise judgment should not be underplayed. In fact, in many cases, it is expertise that allows budget managers and analysts to anticipate events that might be just beyond the horizon. While there are some formal techniques for judgmental forecasting such as the Delphi Technique, Consumer Surveys, Cross-Impact Analysis, and Feasibility Assessment (Dunn, 2012; Stevenson, 2015), incorporating expertise into forecasting processes suggests that those involved in the process recognize it as both science and art (Finkler et al., 2013).

Last, expertise confronts one of the primary limitations to regression and other types of mathematical forecasting. As the mathematical techniques presented earlier assume that the past is a good indicator of the future, they are not fruitful when sharp discontinuities arise. Given that expertise requires one to remain aware of internal and external environments, including this factor provides a solid means of anticipating the future when the past cannot serve as a good guide.

## CONCLUSION

This chapter has covered the basic tools and techniques available to budget managers and analysts when anticipating a future state of events or for examining the consequences of possible courses of action. We have highlighted the fact that, though forecasting is often seen as a technical or procedural exercise, it usefulness lies in the ability to access good data and skills. It also relies heavily on the judgment and assumptions of the individuals working within a specific context. Because the organizational conditions of schools, colleges, and universities can often be idiosyncratic, knowing the local culture, context, and conditions makes forecasts that much more reliable.

Finally, it is always important to remember that though many approaches to forecasting take on formal logical structures that are mathematical in nature, the ability of the forecast to provide useful information is primarily dependent upon the assumptions made about the model and the human judgment that goes into interpreting the results. Regardless of the method employed, there will always be a difference between the true values and the forecasted ones. The job of those responsible with forecasting is to get as close as possible.

## QUESTIONS AND EXERCISES ON
## FORECASTING IN HIGHER EDUCATION

1. Why do higher education administrators and analysts carry out forecasting? What is the use?
2. Why are forecasts always off by some amount? Is this a big problem? Why or why not?

3. How should fiscal administration deal with significant but unforeseen events when forecasting?
4. How does human judgment come into play in higher education forecasting? How is this related to budget philosophy?
5. Using the fictional dataset shown in Table 5.3, and Microsoft Excel if available, forecast and compare the following for both Tuition and Fees per student and State Appropriations per student:
   a. 3-year moving average
   b. 5-year moving average
   c. 3-year weighted moving average
   d. 5-year weighted moving average
   e. 3-year exponential smoothing with a smoothing constant ($\alpha$) of .20 and a difference in actual versus forecasted values for time period 20 of $300.
   f. Explain briefly why moving average, weighted average, and exponential smoothing forecasts differ.
6. Using Microsoft Excel and the dataset in Table 5.3, answer the following for both Tuition and Fees and State Appropriations:
   a. How closely correlated are these two variables related over the entire dataset based on the (Pearson) correlation coefficient?

Table 5.3   Fictional Dataset for Forecasting Exercises

| Period | Tuition and Fees/Student | State Appropriations/ Student | 3-Year Weights | 5-Year Weights |
|--------|--------------------------|-------------------------------|----------------|----------------|
| 1 | 1,492.31 | 2,131.23 | | |
| 2 | 1,898.91 | 2,932.32 | | |
| 3 | 2,129.75 | 3,170.64 | | |
| 4 | 2,405.39 | 4,210.94 | | |
| 5 | 2,438.37 | 4,414.92 | | |
| 6 | 2,747.66 | 4,665.64 | | |
| 7 | 3,656.07 | 4,885.36 | | |
| 8 | 3,996.81 | 4,966.73 | | |
| 9 | 4,039.79 | 5,268.67 | | |
| 10 | 4,166.03 | 5,330.20 | | |
| 11 | 4,468.68 | 5,804.23 | | |
| 12 | 5,195.66 | 5,804.29 | | |
| 13 | 5,720.69 | 6,591.48 | | |
| 14 | 6,034.75 | 6,691.75 | | |
| 15 | 6,087.02 | 6,921.12 | | |
| 16 | 6,303.96 | 7,383.40 | | .10 |
| 17 | 6,310.82 | 7,960.05 | | .15 |
| 18 | 7,679.58 | 7,979.40 | .15 | .20 |
| 19 | 7,811.71 | 7,994.73 | .35 | .25 |
| 20 | 8,329.63 | 8,279.02 | .50 | .30 |
| | | Total Weight | 1.0 | 1.0 |

b. What is the direction of the (Pearson) correlation coefficient's sign? What does this indicate with regard to the relationship? How would this change if the sign were in the opposite direction?

c. Predict a 3-year forecast using the example provided in this chapter.

d. Do the same thing as earlier, but this time use the regression function in Excel.

e. What are some of the limitations of using regression forecasting? How does this relate to curvilinear models?

## NOTES

1. Though not referred to as such, these three qualities are derived from Terenzini's (1999) three tiers of organizational intelligence.

2. The "moving" part in this equation has to do with the fact that the average moves to the next group of periods, be they 3–5, or more. Hence, the average moves to the next group of included periods.

3. It is unlikely that the institution will have .3 Full-Time Equivalents (FTEs); however, for illustrative purposes, we include exact values. In some cases, these values would require rounding for appropriate interpretation.

4. In using this example, the authors are cognizant of the fact that we present only the most typical correlation coefficient measure, Pearson's *r*. Students who are working with discrete data, or, for example, survey data, should take care to use the correct correlation measure such as Spearman's Rho, Cramer's V, or Point-Biserial.

5. It is typical to examine the relationships' statistical significance at the .05 level, but it can also be as high as .10.

6. A good introductory text is provided by Murnane and Willet (2011) titled "Methods Matter."

7. To get to this point, one need simply insert a scatter-plot graph of the data. Once this is done, simply right click on any of the data points in the graph and choose "Add Trendline." Once this option is chosen, a screen similar to that shown in Figure 5.2 will appear, and you can explore the many options that exist for trending the data.

*Phase II*

# DEVELOPING AND OVERSEEING THE TOTAL PROGRAM

With the foundational knowledge discussed in phase I, the aspiring higher education budget manager is now prepared to explore concepts related to developing and overseeing the total operating budget of the institution, program, department, and so on. Specifically, the discussion related to phase II will include a review of the typical budget cycle for higher education institutions. In addition, the concepts of budget oversight, auditing budgets, and variance analysis are presented. These concepts, in conjunction with the foundational material covered in phase I, will empower aspiring higher education budget managers with the expertise necessary to effectively and efficiently manage a budget in a way that maximizes the educational opportunities of all students within the organization.

*Chapter 6*

# The Operating Budget Process and Cycle in Higher Education

Managing budgets is relentless work. There are previous budgets to close as well as current budgets to oversee and, if they were not enough, future budgets requiring development and adoption. Effective budget managers understand and utilize the budget cycle to help them in the development and adoption of future budgets. What is the budget cycle? The budget cycle encompasses the steps taken to create a budget or the process of developing a budget up to the point when the governing board approves the budget. While certainly related, cycles for operating and capital do differ in some significant ways, which are dealt with in this chapter.

Given that at least part of higher education budgets rely on public funds generated through the levying of taxes, those entrusted with managing budgets for public organizations are familiar with the volatility between budgets from one year to the next. As a result of this volatility, budget managers should become familiar with the budget cycle to ensure that all future budgets capture anticipated economic trends and align with the organization's vision, mission, and goals.

The content included in this chapter is designed to provide students of the budgetary process a foundational understanding of the budget cycle. In addition, the material included in this chapter will discuss the components and strategies related to budget building, in higher education, with special emphasis on the contextual factors that should be considered in the process. The chapter concludes with a number of exercises designed to provide students of the budget cycle opportunities to apply the theoretical concepts discussed in the chapter to real situations.

## SOME CONTEXTUAL FACTORS

As noted throughout this text, internal and external environments play a central role in the budgets of colleges and universities. As a result, it is necessary to consider how these forces might impact the budget process and cycle. To examine the possible effects from internal and external changes or shocks, let us consider a few situations.

Institutions can often expect that budgets will improve when the fiscal conditions facing the national, state, and local economy get better (Goldstein, 2012). In Colorado, for example, some institutions saw state support increase as the state's economy began to rebound from the 2008 recession (Serna & Weiler, 2014), although it is nowhere near previous levels. While the impacts of the economic turnaround are more evident in the P-12 system, the fact that institutions saw even a small uptick during this period suggests that higher education budgets remain a concern for state legislatures. Another example comes from the populations attending college.

Changing demographics and increased demand for higher education are two of the most pressing external factors impacting the budget and the work of fiscal managers. As the demographics of the college-going population change and the economy improves, it is likely that colleges and universities see increased demand for higher education. In this scenario, institutions will see enrollments rise and revenues increase. Based on the competitive position of institutions, demographic change coupled with an improving economy could mean that budgets will also become healthier.

However, even with increased demand, another related issue is competition for students. Goldstein (2012) suggests that not only is competition for students already stiff, but for institutions that do not adapt to accommodate more nontraditional students, the impacts of competition may be further accentuated and manifest themselves as budgetary issues.

While economic indicators suggest that conditions are improving, higher education's historical funding patterns suggest that it is perhaps more prudent to consider how to react to situations where funding might be cut or expenditures might increase. For example, a decrease to the state's budget could result in some institutions becoming further dependent on tuition and fee revenue as states themselves grapple with decreased revenues.

Moreover, both those institutions that rely on state funds and those that operate independently of state support must nonetheless confront the shifting nature of expenditures. Technology, facilities maintenance, and human resources are internal expenditures that have decidedly taken on new characteristics (Goldstein, 2012).

To illustrate, technology and facilities maintenance are capital outlays that often require significant resources. And while the funding for the major installation or upgrading of these two expenditure types is dealt with in the capital budget, the day-to-day operation and maintenance is part of the operational budget. In other words, expenditures will increase as these new or improved spaces and networks are brought online (Barr & McClellan, 2011; Goldstein, 2012).

As related to changes in the interplay of external and internal environments, it is unlikely that institutions will only have to confront one of the scenarios presented here. For example, it may be the case that the state has decreased its support, enrollments are rising, and both the technological and physical plant infrastructures are in need of improvements. This scenario is not unusual in college and university budgeting and fiscal administration. The ebbs and flows of the economic and political environments taken together with the internal workings of the institution mean that budgetary decisions will reflect the implicit values of the institution.

Next, let us consider human resources. Administrators should consider the needs of their most important asset: the workforce. Higher education is a personnel heavy industry, and the core mission of institutions is supported by individuals at all levels. Hence, the importance of HR to budget discussions should be evident. Much like the discussions around technology and facilities, the creation of new offices and positions or the hiring of superstar faculty have a direct impact on fiscal administration.

Though the environment that is typically confronted in these situations is an internal one, external market forces may exert sufficient pressure so as to require the institution to respond in order to remain competitive. Again, these pressures and the internal factors surrounding them do not exist in a vacuum. Responding to these matters could come alongside any of the other factors mentioned in this section.

Finally, the goal of this section was to highlight just a few of the contextual factors impacting the fiscal administration of colleges and universities throughout the budget process. As the process and the cycles associated with it are often variable, taking into account the possible factors that might impact an institution will position it better to respond to situations that are both expected and unexpected. Leaders should never forget that in large part budgeting is the reflection and materialization of an institution's goals and identity into action and decisions, and that factoring this into the budget process is important if not vital.

## RESPONDING DURING THE BUDGET PROCESS

There are obviously varied responses to changes that occur during the budget process and cycle. However, before responding leaders overseeing budgets should have clearly defined answers to the following questions prior to having to increase or decrease a budget:

1. What principles guide your decision-making process when developing a budget?
2. What would you not change in a departmental, office, or institutional budget under any circumstance? Why?
3. What would you be willing to add to or cut from a budget? Why?

Because budget philosophy is central to the resource allocation process, an explicit statement or understanding of the principles undergirding decision-making will help make the budget allocation process much easier. This means that before the budget process gets under way, the budget manager should consider which principles will guide decision-making. In higher education this task is not a simple one.

For example, multiple criteria could be used to make a fiscal decision such as: do we wish our decisions to result in equal, equitable, efficient, or some other result? Do we wish for some combination of these? If so, which principles are most important, and how do we compare alternatives? These are just a few questions that might arise as the budget manager makes decisions or compares budgetary outcomes.

The next discussion point should center on the institution's vision statement, mission statement, and goals. In other words, based on the goals of the institution, what are some things that we are unwilling to change or give up? As the budget is the physical representation of the institution's objectives, knowing the answers, or at least considering them, will certainly help make for a smoother budget process.

In lean times, across the board cuts might be considered as part of the process or in times of plenty across the board increases. What arises then is a concern with whether the mission and values of the institution are truly reflected in the budget process and the resulting document. That is to say, clear articulation of why certain resource allocation decisions make sense based on the goals and objectives of the college or university can significantly lighten the workload related to fiscal administration.

One sage piece of advice offered by budget and planning scholars (Barr & McClellan, 2011; Goldstein, 2012) is that regardless of the choices to be made, the human costs and impacts on employee and institutional morale that these decisions engender should always be considered.

Finally, the third point is deciding what the institution is willing to change. While the second and third points may seem redundant, the truth is that providing information on both budgetary decisions that will not change and those that will can provide room for compromise. For example, assume that the core mission of an institution is engineering education. Then perhaps there is a strong interest in maintaining funding to engineering and math programs.

In the same institution, assume that new cost-savings have arisen and that faculty wages have remained frozen for a few years. While the institution might be unwilling to consider cuts to the engineering and math programs, it could compromise by employing these new cost-savings to provide faculty raises while keeping funding to these two programs constant. Again, the impact of these policies on the individuals affected should always be a primary concern.

Finally, the three questions posed at the beginning of this section are likely to be only the first of many that will arise throughout the process. Through each component of the budget cycle, from preparation and adoption, to implementation and evaluation (Finkler et al., 2013), these three questions will likely come up in different iterations and forms. Still, the fundamental questions often remain the same as decisions are made at each stage.

## THE OPERATING BUDGET CYCLE IN HIGHER EDUCATION

In higher education, the budget cycle can take many forms based on the institution's character, identity, size, and control. Hence, we believe it best to explain this process sequentially. Following Barr and McClellan (2011), Finkler et al., (2013), and Goldstein (2012), we break the process up into four distinct stages with a total of fifteen steps (Table 6.1).

The budget cycle for colleges and universities does contain quite a few steps and may appear a bit cumbersome. However, each step exists to ensure that limited resources are efficiently and effectively deployed in support of institutional mission, goals, and values. What is more, the budget cycle as outlined here is a very general one and makes explicit assumptions about timing and process. A primary example of this is in the evaluation steps presented under tasks 14 and 15. The fourth stage, for the most part, is often dealt with in what is known as the thirteenth-month cleanup (Barr & McClellan, 2011) or after the regular fiscal year.

As budget evaluation provides invaluable information regarding operations, it is unwise to wait too long after the close of the fiscal year to examine benchmarks and measures of fiscal performance. These data can provide needed guidance for the next cycle while allowing the institution to remain accountable to the numerous stakeholders in the process (Finkler et al., 2013).

As with any matter of fiscal administration, the role of the budget manager is, again, to know how the local context might require realignment of processes to best serve institutional goals. In other words, while the budget cycle model presented here provides a good heuristic, it is no substitute for

**Table 6.1** Example Budget Cycle for an Institution's Single Fiscal Year

| Stage in Cycle | Tasks | Timeline | Description |
|---|---|---|---|
| Prepare Budget | 1. Plan development | May–June 30 | Using current and past planning information develop current budget plan |
| | 2. Close out prior year | July 1–31 | This time is used to finalize budget adjustments for the previous year |
| | 3. Variance analysis for current year | August–November | Analyze year-to-date results as compared to previous year's final results |
| | 4. Forecast revenues, expenditures, and enrollments | August–November | This period is used to forecast these important values based on planning information and local context |
| | 5. Update strategic plans | November–February | Meet with deans, office, and departmental heads to update strategic priorities |
| | 6. Explicit establishment of budget assumptions for board approval | November–February | Create allocation rules, including modifications impacting budgets, and submit these to the board for approval |
| Adopt and Review Budget | 7. Adopt and distribute budget guidelines | December | Provide budget guidelines and framework to units for budget development |
| | 8. Submit budget proposals | December | Each unit should submit its proposal to the next successive level, until all units have provided a budget to the budget office |
| | 9. Budget hearings and negotiation | December | If hearings and negotiations are part of the institutional budgeting process, participation in these hearings can provide a space for units to make the case for resource requests |

**Table 6.1** (Continued).

| Stage in Cycle | Tasks | Timeline | Description |
|---|---|---|---|
| Adopt and Review Budget | 10. Analyze budget submissions and consolidate full budget | December–January | Once budgets proposals are submitted analysis and consolidation of budgets should occur so as to ensure that each complies with the framework and guidelines provided in step 7 |
| Implement and Monitor Budget | 12. Implement budget | February | Once approved, the budget can be implemented and accounting systems can be updated to reflect new allocations |
| | 13. Monitor budget variances | February–June | Over the implementation phase, fiscal managers must periodically examine variances and make adjustments as appropriate |
| Evaluate Budget | 14. Prepare audited statements | Next fiscal year | This is one of the last stages in the budget phase and includes closing the, now most recent, previous year's financial statements |
| | 15. Examine performance and identify inefficiencies | Next fiscal year | The last element of a budget's cycle is the evaluation of variances and results to help with future planning and decision-making |

contextual knowledge and technical know-how. One the one hand, this model assumes a relatively linear and stepwise process. On the other hand, the reality is that budgets and their related processes vary (Goldstein, 2012).

In fact, one of the primary factors that will impact how budgets are developed, implemented, and finalized is related to the manner in which each part of the process fluctuates based on sometimes very local or more institutional or macro dynamics. Hence, dealing effectively with these fluctuations throughout the budget cycle is one of the foremost concerns for the budget manager.

Another important limitation of the process as outlined in Table 6.1 is that its focus is at the institutional level. This is not to suggest that administrators charged with budget management at the unit level should find this explanation not useful. Rather, as noted earlier, it can still serve as a rather handy heuristic regarding the general tenets of budget development. Moreover, taking into account the processes outlined earlier can provide a "big-picture" view of the budget cycle for the institution from the perspective of unit budgeters. That is to say, given that the underlying goals of the institution should guide budgeting at every level, this perspective can provide guidance regarding resource allocation decisions at every point within the institution.

A third, and related, limitation is that this exposition of the budget cycle does not explicitly deal with the nuances and timing of state legislative processes. That is to say, especially for public colleges and universities, the role of the state is only implicitly considered and hence, fiscal administration should clearly account for ebbs and flows of state legislative cycles As stated before, this is where the role of the budget manager is especially important. A firm grasp of the legislative impacts likely to affect budgeting and planning at the institution can provide valuable decision-making information.

Finally, it is important to point out that the process outlined in this chapter is focused on the operating budget. And though the operating budget is certainly impacted by decisions around capital projects and acquisitions, the discussion of capital budgets is left to chapters 8 and 9.

## CONCLUSION

In closing this chapter it is necessary to underscore how familiarity with the sequence of the budget process and progression of the budget cycle are related to successful fiscal administration. A working knowledge of the process in both this more abstract form and in context is vital for new budget managers. To be sure, the stages and tasks highlighted in this chapter can be adapted to just about any office, unit, department, or institution with relative ease.

In addition to this, understanding how multiple circumstances intersect to form the budget environment provides invaluable decision-making information throughout the process and cycle. With the information provided in this chapter, new and current budget managers no doubt have at their disposal the proper tools to take budgets under their supervision from preparation through evaluation stages.

## QUESTIONS ABOUT THE OPERATING BUDGETING PROCESS

1. What are the fundamental differences between operating and capital budgets? Why are they different?
2. How closely does the process outlined here reflect practices in your unit, office, program, institution, and/or department? How does this process relate to day-to-day activities?
3. How should decision-makers make tradeoffs during the budgeting cycle? What are some typical responses to tight budgets?
4. Why does the adage "budgeting is always happening" ring true for colleges and universities?
5. How can budget philosophy impact the operating budgeting cycle and its related processes?

*Chapter 7*

# Oversight and Budget Variance Analysis

An important part of examination and oversight of institutional performance is to analyze the variance between forecasted and actual numbers. While we note in chapter 3 that a small variance is likely, large variances could indicate some trouble with the analytic approach, data, or assumptions. In this chapter, we outline techniques that allow the budget manager to examine variances and provide some guidance for dealing with them to improve oversight.

Based on the rather cyclical nature of revenue and expenditure patterns, knowing when and in what part of the budget to expect variances will help budget managers provide useful information to those charged with budget oversight. Additionally, we briefly examine the role that accounting standards play in understanding budget variances and how this can impact the decision-making process as well as the role of auditing in budget oversight.

## VARIANCES IN REVENUES AND EXPENDITURES

For budget oversight to be effective, it must systematically examine whether forecasts are within a reasonable range when compared to observed revenues and expenditures. A first step to this process is to examine the budget in parts. While the budget itself and budgeting are often treated as a single document or process, the reality is that even related subcomponents can differ widely from one another (Finkler et al., 2013).

By examining components and subcomponents that are linked or reported together, it is possible to determine whether one part of the budget or related areas make up the largest variances. It may be the case that a large variance is being caused by faulty forecasts in only one part of the budget. By examining variances systematically and in parts, the budget manager can be assured that valuable time and resources are not being used inefficiently (Finkler et al., 2013).

Finally, because forecasting allows us to make decisions about the future states of affairs, we should wish to make variances between the forecasted and observed values as small as possible. Knowing where in the budget large variances occur is only the first step. The next step is to determine if these variances are a result of the cyclical nature of education finance or if structural elements have changed resulting in a need to rethink forecasting assumptions.

## OVERSIGHT AND THE ROLE OF CYCLICAL AND STRUCTURAL VARIANCES

In the budget oversight process, an important distinction to make when examining the difference between observed and forecasted values is whether the resulting variance is due to cyclical forces or a structural change. When variances are due to a change in the budget environment that is either anticipated or that happens on a regular basis, budget managers should focus attention on how best to deal with the variance based on historical knowledge and local context.

Usually, a good course of action for cyclical budget variances is to reference policy for these anticipated fluctuations. In the event that a policy is not in place, the development of budget stabilization policies should look to smooth revenues or expenditures over this time so as to minimize differences between actual and anticipated values. Additionally, prudent use of cash reserves when available could help mitigate some of the difficulties that arise when cyclical variances occur.

If smoothing is not an option, then budget managers should try to anticipate which time periods will result in higher revenues or increased expenditures based on the business cycle. For example, while a budget manager may not be able to anticipate perfectly a state reduction in funding or when it might occur, having a plan for dealing with a significant difference between forecasted and actual funds is wise and should be based on information regarding state support in the past.

In other words, examining variances in revenues and expenditures from previous periods based on contextual knowledge of previous funding cycles and levels could provide a guide for dealing with budget fluctuations. Once again, the use of cash reserves in an appropriate fashion could alleviate some of the pressures that build when variances occur. For example, it may be the case that reserves have been used in a similar way in previous periods, and this can provide some guidance for the current period. In fact, the techniques presented in this chapter can be employed in the examination of the use and cyclicality of cash reserves as well.

Another good example of seasonal cyclicality comes from physical plant maintenance. Say, for example, that utility costs are estimated based on a twelve-month figure, so that the value for each month is the same. However, it is more likely that utility costs will be higher during the time period that the physical plant is used most. In this instance, the budget manager might have negative variances for, say, nine months and positive variances for three months. Locally, the reasons for this are clear; however, when a budget document is examined as a whole, these variances might raise questions. As the budget manager knows that the cyclical nature of the physical plant's use accounts for this, she is in a position to mitigate concerns that the organization is running deficits some months and surpluses in others.

Now let's turn to structural variances. Structural variances arise when there is a change to the actual structure of the budget, its rules, or its policy. They differ from cyclical variances in that they are related to the structure of the budget process rather than to its fluctuations. A good example of this for higher education comes from changes in the accounting standards from the financial and governmental accounting boards (FASB and GASB) (McKeown-Moak & Mullin, 2014). For example, the changed rules required two sets of accounting. GASB rules required public institutions to report two sets of revenue categories as "operating" and "nonoperating" revenues whereas FASB rules required no such distinction. While this may not seem a highly important distinction, the methods for reporting revenues and expenditures based on whether the institution follows GASB or FASB rules could differ considerably.

In other words, variance analysis could indicate very different values based on the structural requirements and embedded assumptions of the budget process. Therefore, it is prudent for budget managers to understand clearly whether the variances they estimate are of a cyclical nature or a structural one. Speaking directly to the subject of cash reserves, in this case, they usually provide a buffer during the time period when policy, budgeting, or organizational changes must be made to deal with new structural constraints and opportunities. It is usually ill-advised to assume that cash reserves can shield the institution from structural changes over the long run.

## VARIANCE ANALYSIS USING SUMMARY MEASURES

In this section, we outline the most common methods for examining variances among forecasted revenues and costs when compared to actual values using summary measures of the error. The exposition of these methods is

Table 7.1    Hypothetical Dataset with Actual, Forecasted, and Variance for Tuition and
Fees

| Period | Tuition and Fees Actual (ya) | Tuition and Fees Forecast (yf) | Variance (ya − yf) | Variance Squared (ya − yf)$^2$ | Absolute Value of Variance \|e\| |
|---|---|---|---|---|---|
| 1 | 1989.20 | 1904.89 | 84.31 | 7108.18 | 84.31 |
| 2 | 3198.75 | 3157.22 | 41.54 | 1725.57 | 41.54 |
| 3 | 3312.53 | 3841.08 | −528.55 | 279365.10 | 528.55 |
| 4 | 3326.74 | 3131.44 | 195.30 | 38412.09 | 195.30 |
| 5 | 3399.78 | 3705.05 | −305.26 | 93183.67 | 305.26 |
| 6 | 3533.82 | 3796.14 | −262.32 | 68811.78 | 262.32 |
| 7 | 4706.70 | 4946.81 | −240.11 | 57652.81 | 240.11 |
| 8 | 5248.03 | 5039.94 | 208.09 | 43301.45 | 208.09 |
| 9 | 5306.23 | 5288.59 | 17.64 | 311.17 | 17.64 |
| 10 | 5363.51 | 6640.95 | −1277.44 | 1631852.95 | 1277.44 |
| 11 | 5403.13 | 5966.97 | −563.84 | 317915.55 | 563.84 |
| 12 | 5833.94 | 6031.24 | −197.30 | 38927.29 | 197.30 |
| 13 | 5833.94 | 5701.17 | 132.76 | 17625.22 | 132.76 |
| 14 | 6221.86 | 6850.37 | −628.50 | 395012.25 | 628.50 |
| 15 | 6514.96 | 7040.69 | −525.72 | 276381.52 | 525.72 |
| 16 | 6734.66 | 6318.84 | 415.82 | 172906.27 | 415.82 |
| 17 | 7029.66 | 7051.69 | −22.02 | 484.88 | 22.02 |
| 18 | 7755.49 | 7835.65 | −80.16 | 6425.63 | 80.16 |
| 19 | 8359.46 | 8969.99 | −610.53 | 372746.88 | 610.53 |
| 20 | 8903.04 | 9101.90 | −198.87 | 39549.28 | 198.87 |
| Σ | 107975.45 | 112320.61 | −4345.16 | 3859429.54 | 6536.08 |

guided by examples from Dunn (2012), Stevenson (2015), and Trochim and
Donnelly (2007). By providing perspectives from three areas, policy analysis,
operations management, and statistics, we are able to provide a step-by-step
guide for carrying out typical variance analyses for just about any budget
manager needing summary measures of forecast accuracy. It should be noted
that because the measures employ error as a summary measure of forecasting
accuracy, the goal is always to have smaller, rather than larger, variances. For
the examples in this chapter, we will use the preceding hypothetical dataset
for tuition and fees over the past twenty time periods (Table 7.1).[1]

## Standard Error of Estimate

The standard error of estimate, or $S_e$, is a measure of the accuracy of prediction when using regression analysis for forecasting. It allows the budget
manager to determine whether data points for both the actual and forecasted
values are closely scattered near the line of best fit. The first step in this
process is to plot the values and then impose a linear trend based on the forecasted results as shown in Figure 7.1.

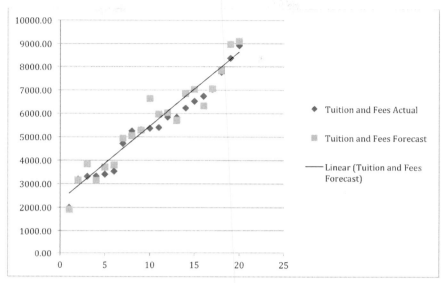

**Figure 7.1   Scatter Plot of Actual and Forecasted Tuition and Fee Values with Linear Trend Superimposed.** *Source*: Authors.

This simple scatter plot shows that the forecasted and actual values move in a relatively similar fashion to one another and are rather closely grouped around the line of best fit. As noted in chapter 5, this should be done before forecasting as well to determine if a linear forecasting trend makes sense. In this case it does. While this graphic shows us that the scatter appears close to the line, we may want to be able to quantify this in dollar terms to determine how far off the estimate is based on the distance between the actual and forecasted values. The standard error of estimate is calculated using the following equation (Stevenson, 2015, p. 103; Dunn, 2012, p. 103), where a sample of time periods has been taken as in our example:

$$S_e = \sqrt{\frac{\sum(y_a - y_f)^2}{n-2}}.$$

Here, the actual tuition and fee values $(y_a)$ are subtracted from the forecasted ones $(y_f)$, squared, and then summed, in that order.[2] The numerator is then divided by the total number of observations $(n)$ minus two. We then take the square root of this value for an estimate of the standard error. We should highlight that when calculating the $S_e$ with an entire population of values (every period), it is not necessary to divide by $n - 2$ but rather only by $n$ (Dunn, 2012).[3]

Now let us make this a bit more concrete using our dataset from above. If we take this equation and plug in values from Table 7.1, where we first subtract each actual value from the forecasted value and square the result, the equation is:

$$S_e = \sqrt{\frac{(3,859,429.54)}{20-2}} = 463.05.$$

To interpret this statistic, we need to construct a probability interpretation. So using a 95% confidence level, which is typical, the $S_e$ tell us that 95% of the time we are within +/926.10 tuition and fee dollars of the mean observed value.[4] The power of this technique is highlighted by Dunn (2012, p. 162):

> The standard error of estimate allows us to make estimates that take error into account. Rather than make simple point estimates—that is, estimates that yield values of $Y_c$ [Forecasted values of Y]—we can make interval estimates that yield values of $Y_c$ expressed in terms of one or more standard units of error.

In other words, we can expect forecasts to be within this range, above, or below the actual mean of tuition and fees a certain percentage of the time. Additionally, while the current example employs a revenue source for exposition, this applies equally well to expenditure forecasts, enrollments, and so on.

The first question that probably comes to mind is whether this is acceptable, large, or small. The reality is it depends. In this example, the $S_e$ suggests that the deviation from the mean is not so large. Especially since the mean of the actual values is equal to 5398.77. This indicates that it is likely that the forecasting assumptions and model are working well. What is more, the $S_e$ is directly related to the mean of observed values and thus, contextual knowledge about what may be large, small, or acceptable is vital. This again underscores the important role of human judgment in tandem with sophisticated methods to obtain worthwhile forecasts (Finkler et al., 2013).

To be clear, the usefulness of the $S_e$ lies in its ability to help the budget manager determine if forecasts and actual values are closely grouped because it depends on a more sophisticated forecasting approach (regression analysis) to determine the next forecasted value. It also expresses numerically the interval of error (at a 95% confidence level) that can be expected most of the time when predicting revenues and expenditures. Therefore, coupling local knowledge with appropriate forecasting approaches and assumptions can provide the budget manager essential information for decision-making and resource deployment.

## Mean Absolute Deviation

The mean absolute deviation, or MAD, is the average absolute forecast error (Stevenson, 2015, p. 81). It is the absolute value of the difference between each value and the mean of the dataset. So in general the equation for calculating the MAD is (Stevenson, 2015, p. 81):

$$MAD = \frac{\sum |e|}{n}.$$

Where the *e* within the two brackets is the absolute value of the error (actual values minus forecasted values) divided by the total number of data points (*n*). To illustrate, let us use the data from Table 7.1 with the last six periods (15–20). Based on the information from the table, it is easy to see that the difference between each forecast and the actual value has been calculated in column four, and the absolute values of these numbers in column five which must be calculated before proceeding. Because the bottom row of Table 7.1 includes these values for all twenty periods, we will have to calculate the MAD for the last six periods. To do so we set up our equation as follows using data from the last column containing the absolute variance values:

$$MAD = \frac{525.72 + 415.82 + 22.02 + 80.16 + 610.53 + 198.87}{6} = 308.853.$$

This value, 308.853, provides a measure of average absolute distance between the data points and the mean of the sample. When the MAD is large, it indicates that the data points are more scattered around the mean, and when small that they are more closely clustered around the mean. As underscored earlier, closer clustering around the mean suggests that forecasts are more accurate. Given that this measure is a mean measure of the error, it is again necessary to determine what large and small mean in context.

In this example, a MAD of 308.853 for the actual value of tuition and fees could suggest that observable variances are relatively small given that the actual values range from a high of 8,903.04 to a low of 6,514.96. Hence, this may indicate that forecasting assumptions are acceptable. However, if, say, we compared the value 308.853 to a high of 890.30 and a low of 651.49, then this MAD would be rather large and could indicate that a revisiting forecasting assumptions is required. Finally, it is important to note that this approach is relatively simple to employ; however, it also makes assumptions about the error. Namely, it weights the error linearly, which imposes a strict assumption about forecasted values (Stevenson, 2015).

## Mean Squared Error

In terms of summarizing the accuracy of a forecast, the mean squared error or MSE, is often considered to be one of the most powerful tools at an analyst's disposal. It is very good measure of the precision and accuracy of a forecast based on historical data (SAS/STAT(R), 2009). In mathematical terms, it is denoted by the following equation (Stevenson, 2015, p. 81):

$$MSE = \frac{\sum e^2}{n-1}.$$

In this equation, the MSE is equal to the sum of the squared errors[5] divided by the number of observations minus one. For example, if we use the same tuition and fee data as in the previous example with six periods, the equation would take the following form again using the absolute values of the forecast error:

$$MSE = \frac{525.72^2 + 415.82^2 + 22.02^2 + 80.16^2 + 610.53^2 + 198.87^2}{5} = 173,698.89.$$

Now this number may seem enormous and, in fact, it is. Therefore, a good approach is simply to take the square root of the MSE to obtain the root mean squared error (RMSE). By doing so we can interpret the MSE in the original units. So in this example, that would mean taking the SqRt(173,698.89) for a value of 416.77. This is then interpreted in the original units (tuition and fee dollars) and used in much the same way as the MAD when comparing the RMSE to the actual values to determine if it is too large or too small (Vernier, 2011), but as always larger numbers mean more forecasting inaccuracy. It should be highlighted that the RMSE is also used in control charts, which are explained here, to provide both tracking information and visual information related to forecast accuracy.

This method is very useful and can provide a sophisticated summary measure of the forecast variance. However, like other methods, it also suffers from a rather important limitation. Primarily that the use of squared errors results in larger weights for larger errors so that when the difference between the actual and forecasted values are large, these values are given heavier weighting. This can lead to problems with both precision and bias in forecast estimates and hence should be considered carefully when using this approach (SAS/STAT(R), 2009; Stevenson, 2015).

## Mean Absolute Percentage Error

The mean absolute percentage error, or MAPE, is the value of the average absolute percent error. Essentially, this measures forecasting accuracy in percentage terms as opposed to original units. The equation for calculating the MAPE is (Stevenson, 2015, p. 81):

Table 7.2   Hypothetical Dataset with Actual, Forecasted, Variance, and Percentages*

| Period | Tuition and Fees Actual (ya) | Tuition and Fees Forecast (yf) | Variance (ya – yf) | Absolute Value of Variance \|e\| | (\|e\| ÷ ya) × 100 |
|---|---|---|---|---|---|
| 15 | 6514.96 | 7040.69 | –525.72 | 525.72 | 8.07% |
| 16 | 6734.66 | 6318.84 | 415.82 | 415.82 | 6.17% |
| 17 | 7029.66 | 7051.69 | –22.02 | 22.02 | 0.31% |
| 18 | 7755.49 | 7835.65 | –80.16 | 80.16 | 1.03% |
| 19 | 8359.46 | 8969.99 | –610.53 | 610.53 | 7.30% |
| 20 | 8903.04 | 9101.9 | –198.87 | 198.87 | 2.23% |
| | | | | Σ = | 25.13% |

*Readers should note that some calculations may be off by a slight amount because of rounding errors that occur when only two decimal places are used for presentation, but the equation employs up to eight decimal places.

$$MAPE = \frac{\sum[\frac{|e|}{y_a} \times 100]}{n}.$$

Here the numerator is equal to the sum of the absolute values of the error terms ($e$) divided by the actual forecast for each included period multiplied by 100. So let us assume that we will do this again for the last six periods from the dataset in Table 7.1. The calculations would look like the values in Table 7.2.

The values in the last column of Table 7.2 are calculated by taking the absolute variance value ($|e|$) from each time period and dividing it by its corresponding actual values ($y_a$). Therefore, to obtain the value 8.07% for time period 15, we simply calculate (525.72/6,514.96) × 100. The same is done for each time period. So for period 16, the equation to be calculated would be (415.82/6,734.66) × 100 = 6.17%. Once we have calculated all of these values for each time period, they are summed and we have the value 25.13%. In order to obtain the MAPE, we simply plug in these values as such:

$$MAPE = \frac{25.13\%}{6} = 4.19\%.$$

The resulting value of 4.19% suggests that our forecast is off by a little over 4% for the periods included in the calculation. This does not appear to be a very large amount, and based on previous calculations of the MSE and MAD, it would seem that the budget manager is doing a rather good job at forecasting future tuition and fee revenues.[6]

As has been highlighted in previous sections, summary measures of forecast accuracy provide a great deal of useful information and the MAPE is not different in this sense. It provides information that can put the error in perspective (Stevenson, 2015) so that errors are understood in percentage terms rather than simply units. It does, however, suffer from a rather important limitation. Chiefly being that it does not deal well with near-zero or actual zero values. This is a result of its mechanics, which render the value of the MAPE undefined.

## A Visual Approach to Oversight and Monitoring of Forecast Variance

In the previous section, the goal was to outline the most common methods for examining forecast variance using summary measures of the error. In this section, we outline the most common method for tracking forecast variance rather than simply measuring it. Following Stevenson (2015), we provide detailed examples and step-by-step instructions for using a *control chart* approach. As in the previous section, the examples used here employ the hypothetical dataset for tuition and fees over the last twenty time periods presented in Table 7.1 with a few changes based on what is needed for each approach.

We should also underscore that we have chosen not to provide a detailed exposition of another method for monitoring forecast accuracy, *tracking signal*, because recent advances in computing power have resulted in the use of the more sophisticated approach presented in this section. Moreover, using a tracking signal to examine forecast accuracy is severely limited by its focus on cumulative rather than individual errors. The approach does not consider each error individually but rather relies on cumulative values that can obscure individual outliers important to the analysis (Stevenson, 2015).

### Control Chart

This method is used for tacking forecast accuracy by identifying possible nonrandomness in forecasting errors (Stevenson, 2015). By using the equivalent of what would be the mean for an error (0) and standard deviation-mean square error, the control chart provides a visual and sophisticated means of tracking errors using the basic probabilities outlined in the section titled "Standard Error of Estimate" (see footnote 3). Because we assume that this is a sample of possible periods, when calculating the MSE we should use the $n - 1$ convention to help reduce bias in our estimates.

The computation and creation of a control chart requires a great deal of data and computing assistance. Using Excel, this task becomes much easier.[7] For example, in Figure 7.2 a control chart example is provided in an Excel screenshot.

To start with, the budget manager will need to calculate the MSE using the technique presented earlier in this chapter and take its square root ($s$).

**Table 7.3  Control Chart Data**

| Period | Variance (Error) | Error Squared |
|--------|------------------|---------------|
| 1 | 84.31 | 7108.82 |
| 2 | 41.54 | 1725.22 |
| 3 | −528.55 | 279365.25 |
| 4 | 195.30 | 38142.93 |
| 5 | −305.26 | 93184.73 |
| 6 | −262.32 | 68812.83 |
| 7 | −240.11 | 57652.91 |
| 8 | 208.09 | 43302.73 |
| 9 | 17.64 | 311.23 |
| 10 | −1277.44 | 1631843.21 |
| 11 | −563.84 | 317912.89 |
| 12 | −197.30 | 38927.99 |
| 13 | 132.76 | 17626.02 |
| 14 | −628.50 | 395016.38 |
| 15 | −525.72 | 276385.99 |
| 16 | 415.82 | 172905.37 |
| 17 | −22.02 | 485.08 |
| 18 | −80.16 | 6425.20 |
| 19 | −610.53 | 372752.06 |
| 20 | −198.87 | 39547.50 |
| | Σ | *3859434.35* |
| | *MSE* | *203128.12* |
| | *RMSE* | *450.70* |

This measure works similar to the computation of a standard deviation but is specifically for measuring the distribution of error terms. So again following Stevenson's approach (p. 107) we need to compute the following values:

$$s = \sqrt{MSE}.$$

$$Upper\,Control\,Limit\,(UCL) = 0 + z * s.$$

$$Lower\,Control\,Limit\,(LCL) = 0 - z * s.$$

Here $s$ is equal to the square root of the MSE, and $z$ is equal to the number of standard deviations away from the mean (of the error values) that are statistically acceptable assuming normality of the distribution. So, in this case, 68% of errors are expected to fall within one standard deviation, 95% within two standard deviations, and 99% within three. In other words, the budget manager must set the "limit" on what is acceptably within the upper and lower limits. So in the example provided in Figure 7.2, first we calculate the square root of the MSE, which results in:

$$s = \sqrt{203,128.12} = 450.70.$$

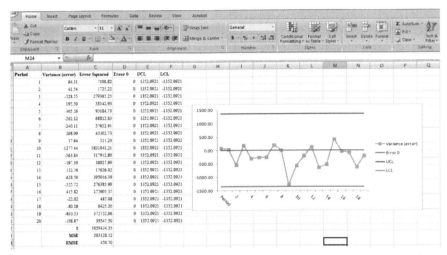

**Figure 7.2    Excel Screen Shot of Data Requirements for Control Chart.** *Source*: Authors.

the UCL limit is calculated with three standard deviations as:

$$UCL = 0 + 3(450.70) = 1,352.0921 \ or \ 1,352.1.$$

and the LCL:

$$LCL = 0 - 3(450.70) = -1,352.0921 \ or \ -1,352.1.$$

This information is then plotted as seen in Figure 7.3. The reason for plotting these values is that it quickly shows that tuition and fees, from a statistically significant perspective, are within acceptable limits if three standard deviations are used. If instead two standard deviations were considered to be the limit, then we would use the same equations and come up with ± 901.40. To help make this clearer, let us turn to deciphering Figure 7.3.

In Figure 7.3, we see four lines on the graph. The darkest line at the top near 1,500 is the UCL, the lighter line near the bottom (−1,500) is the LCL, and the line in the straight line in the middle is the center of the range of random variability based on a normal distribution. The jagged line with the squares is the one connecting each of our variance or error values. Now it is important to emphasize again what the control chart shows; namely, it provides visual information about the spread of forecasting errors. Based on the control chart presented in Figure 7.3, it is clear that all values fall within the UCL and LCL, though one comes pretty close to being beyond the lower limit. While this is good news, the reality is that we must consider not only the limits, but the shape of the line as well. The UCL and LCL are only one

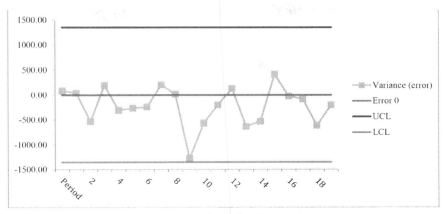

**Figure 7.3   Control Chart Using Hypothetical Tuition and Fee Data.** *Source*: Example adapted from Stevenson, 2015.

measure of the spread of forecasting error. Other things to look for include trends in the variance line, cycling, and bias (Stevenson, 2015).

For example, there does not appear to be any discernible trend either upward or downward, but cycles do seem to be at play here. This could indicate that during certain times, our forecasts are off in a cyclical pattern suggesting that we may not be considering important external factors such as changes in political dynamics around education finance, or increased competition from other institutions.

Additionally, the control chart shows that many of our forecasting errors fall below the centerline. This suggests that our forecasting estimates are biased upward (e.g., actual T&F = 10, 500, forecasted T&F = 11,600, variance is 1,100) and that the budget manager may need to reexamine the internal and external environments as well as the assumptions going into each forecast for changes impacting actual versus forecasted values.

## AUDIT, ACCOUNTABILITY, AND TRANSPARENCY

Another important function of budget oversight and variance analysis is related to accountability and transparency. Finkler et al. (2013, p. 287) note that safeguarding resources is an important function of the oversight process and provide four items that should be considered as both part of the oversight and the audit process, which are summarized here:

1. A management authorization system should be in place so that key activities are carried out only with proper management approval.

2. After authorization is secured, all budgetary and financial transactions should be carefully recorded in preparation for financial statements and to ensure accountability for all resources and assets.
3. Only those with proper management authority should have access to assets and resources.
4. Reconciliation of current assets and resources, and those recorded previously, should occur on a regular basis and differences should be reconciled.

These are clearly only the most basic components of an audit system[8] and set the foundation for a comprehensive audit trail; however, they are extremely important. Moreover, the public nature of higher education means that transparency around financial and budget administration is essential.

As noted by Barr and McClellan (2011), oversight of budgets and audits can come from both internal and external sources. For example, many institutions choose to conduct internal audits to maintain proper oversight and adherence to the audit and control system in place. Additionally, public institutions, as part of their mission to be accountable to taxpayers, are often audited by the state. Institutions that take part in federal grant or student financial aid programs are often required to undergo an audit by the federal government[9] (Goldstein, 2012). Similarly, just about every institution is required to undergo an audit conducted by an external agency. This helps to ensure that a review of institutional fiscal operations and administration is carried out independently.

Finally, while the audit process is typically intended to provide information about appropriate resources management, highlight weaknesses in the process, and strengthen budget procedures, the results of an audit are not necessarily confined to internal uses (Barr & McClellan, 2011). In fact, for public institutions state-level audits are often made public for the sake of transparency and accountability. Hence, the publicness of audits means that the institution should take special care to steer clear of preventable inaccuracies that result from poor oversight or careless budgetary procedures (Barr & McClellan, 2011). While we have underscored the extra scrutiny faced by public institutions, in reality, all institutions should heed the advice provided here.

## CONCLUSION

Analysis of budget variances and appropriate oversight are central components of strong fiscal administration. This chapter has provided myriad examples and methods for examining budget variances. It has also highlighted the important role of oversight and its relationship to accountability and transparency. Because higher education serves a public function, scrutiny of fiscal operations should not be avoided. Indeed, special care must be taken to guarantee that resources and assets are safeguarded and that they are being used appropriately. In this chapter, we have provided the budget manager the tools to do so.

## QUESTIONS AND EXERCISES ON VARIANCE ANALYSIS

1. What general purpose does variance analysis serve in the fiscal administration of higher education institutions?
2. Briefly describe how structural variances and cyclical variances differ from one another.
3. Using the dataset in Table 7.4, and Microsoft Excel if available, calculate each of the following summary measures for all twenty periods:
   a. Standard error of estimate
   b. Mean average deviation
   c. Mean square error
   d. Root mean square error
   e. Mean absolute percentage error
   f. Briefly describe how each measure should be understood
4. Using Microsoft Excel and the dataset provided, create a control chart. Then answer the following questions:

**Table 7.4   Fictional Dataset for Variance Analysis**

| Period | Tuition and Fees Actual (ya) | Tuition and Fees Forecasted (yf) |
|---|---|---|
| 1 | 2557.46 | 2172.85 |
| 2 | 2688.30 | 2207.55 |
| 3 | 3245.73 | 2678.30 |
| 4 | 3921.61 | 3040.08 |
| 5 | 3931.01 | 3378.16 |
| 6 | 4281.08 | 3412.76 |
| 7 | 4560.28 | 3433.83 |
| 8 | 5064.07 | 3920.62 |
| 9 | 5637.17 | 5133.58 |
| 10 | 5745.11 | 5430.68 |
| 11 | 6024.17 | 5890.37 |
| 12 | 6494.71 | 6381.77 |
| 13 | 6495.92 | 6441.94 |
| 14 | 7227.13 | 6644.68 |
| 15 | 7806.97 | 7155.74 |
| 16 | 7981.96 | 7163.57 |
| 17 | 8167.25 | 8470.78 |
| 18 | 8348.33 | 8775.48 |
| 19 | 8453.10 | 8817.68 |
| 20 | 8684.09 | 9082.85 |

a. What does the visualization of data in the control charts represent?
b. How does one go about interpreting the information?
c. When should a budget manager become concerned by the data presented in a control chart?
d. What if the control chart shows that values are close to, but not outside, the threshold limits? How might a new budget manager approach this?
e. What if limits are only reached, or closely reached, for one time period? Should a full reexamination take place? What if this instead is happening consistently?

5. Briefly describe the fundamental components of an appropriate audit process.
   a. Describe how human judgment plays a role in forecasting for institutions of higher education.

## NOTES

1. Periods can be any length of time, including, day, week, month, semester, trimester, or year.

2. Readers should note that not following the proper order of operations will result in a very different and incorrect value for the numerator of the $S_e$.

3. Trochim and Donnelly (2007) suggest dividing by $n - 1$ instead of $n - 2$. However, the goal of both of these corrections is to estimate unbiased standard errors.

4. This value is calculated by multiplying the $S_e$ by the number of standard deviations related to the interval where the forecast will be roughly within one standard deviation of the actual mean 68% of the time, within two standard deviations 95% of the time, and within three standard deviations 99% of the time. So we simply multiply $463.05 \times 2$ to construct the probability interpretation.

5. Readers may be confused by the fact that we do not employ the absolute value in this equation. The reason for doing so is that squaring the value of $e$ results in positive numbers, which is the same logic behind using absolute values.

6. The appropriate measure of MAPE values is based on local context and depends greatly on the requirements of the organization. In some instances, a MAPE of less than 5% is acceptable whereas in other instances, a MAPE of less than 20% is acceptable.

7. For those unfamiliar with Excel for control charts a great video tutorial exists from Eugene O'Loughlin (2012) at the National College of Ireland at https://www.youtube.com/watch?v=zvp8qmH3Eos using examples that are readily adaptable to the exercises presented here.

8. For a detailed description of the element of a control system, see Finkler et al. (2013, pp. 287–93).

9. Goldstein (2012, p. 18) highlights the fact that Office of Management and Budget (OMB) Circulars A-110 and A-133 govern the process for the audit of federally funded programs.

*Phase III*

# FOUNDATIONS OF CAPITAL BUDGETING AND USING DEBT

In this phase of the book, we present some other important budget components and considerations. Specifically, we are interested in providing readers with an overview of the capital budgeting process, both with and without debt, time value of money basics, and cost–benefit analysis tools. We then move on to the role of the strategic plan in budgeting and see how the aggregation of both the operating and capital budgets constitutes the "master budget." This master budget is highly influential in the planning process because it outlines the overall goals and objectives of the institution in financial terms. What is more, the master budget is a manifestation of the previous planning processes and a starting point for future plans. It is the relationship between budgets and planning that is the focus of chapter 10. The final chapter of this phase offers some concluding remarks and perspectives on major trends in the field and on the role of budgeting and fiscal management in the larger landscape of higher education.

# Chapter 8

# Capital Budgets without Debt

The capital budget serves to facilitate the acquisition and financial management of long-term physical assets and other assets that last for more than one operating year (Finkler et al., 2013; Lee, Johnson, & Joyce, 2013). In higher education, the majority of capital budgets deal with the maintenance, renovation, repair, replacement, or new construction of physical plant (buildings, classrooms, lab space, student centers, etc.) or other large expenditures such as vehicles for a motor pool or new technology for enrollment management or campus in general (Barr & McClellan, 2011).

They are also closely related to college and university marketing as a tool to help institutions differentiate themselves from competitors. For example, Jacob, Stange, and McCall (2013) and Serna (2013b, c) suggest that capital investments in nonacademic, lifestyle activities are becoming the norm on many campuses. In order to pay for these amenities and other large capital acquisitions, colleges and universities must use capital budgets to plan how funds will be allocated across these activities over many years.

So why is a separate budget needed to deal with these types of expenditures? Well, the capital budget allows for institutions to amortize the cost of these asset types over the useful life of the asset through a process called amortization (Finkler et al., 2013). This process means that institutional finances do not take a huge "hit" when large dollar items are required. In other words, the amortization principle allows for fiscal managers to budget the day-to-day operation of the asset over a longer period of time and account only for related costs to be included in the operating budget under "depreciation" in the financial statements (Finkler et al., 2013).

This is done so long as the asset remains useful or in operation. What is more this process means that many future time periods are part of the budgeting process when dealing with capital assets. Finally, the institution must set guidelines regarding dollar limits for those items to be included in the capital budget. For example, Finkler et al. (2013, p. 165) suggest that capital expenditures should typically require a significant outlay of resources and be useful and owned for a long period of time.

Generally speaking, the capital budgeting process includes only six steps as outlined by Goldstein (2012, pp. 129–31) and presented in Table 8.1 in three stages. It is important to note that while the focus of this chapter is on capital budgeting without debt, the same process holds for capital budgeting with debt. For example, in presenting discounting and compounding rates and process, both are related to the coupon rates for bond debt. Indeed, bond-valuation requires estimating cash flows and presented discounted values for a bond similar to those presented in this chapter.

Additionally, the same notions around the useful life and policies for determining what should be considered a capital asset apply. As can be seen in Table 8.1, when compared with the operating budget, the capital budget cycle has fewer stages and steps; however, one should not take this to indicate that the budget cycle is less complicated or shorter. In fact, as compared with the operating budget, the capital budget deals with fiscal administration and budgeting over a much longer period of years (Goldstein, 2012).

While Table 8.1 provides a broad overview of the process, as with other budgeting and financial decisions, the local context should always be considered. That is to say, as with the ebbs and flows related to the operating budget, both internal and external factors impacting the process should be considered when undertaking capital budgeting. In addition, the process outlined here points to an important part of the capital budget process—that the financial impact of large acquisitions is only truly understood over the useful life of the asset. Because this is the case, the time value of money (TVM) plays an important role in determining the best use of capital funds (Finkler et al., 2013; Johnson et al., 2013).

Another important part of the capital budgeting process that is not included in Table 8.1 is the relationship of the capital budget to the operating budget. While the process outlined earlier explains how the acquisition of big-ticket items proceeds, it does little to tell us about the impact of capital investments and acquisitions on the other part of the "master budget," the operating side. For the most part, capital budgets impact operating budgets in at least three ways.

First, there are often operating costs associated with increased faculty or staff when a project is completed. This directly impacts the operating budget by increasing the day-to-day costs of running campus. Second, once the project is brought online, it will require maintenance funding. While many capital projects require some reserve to deal with this part of the process, it is not always the case that these will cover the full costs of operation especially

**Table 8.1** Example Operating Budget Cycle for an Institution over Four Fiscal Years

| Stage in Cycle | Task | Timeline (Fiscal Year July 1–June 30) | Description |
|---|---|---|---|
| Space Needs and Campus Plans | 1. Determine space requirements | Fiscal Year 1 | This part of the process should occur at the department, office, or program level and include a rationale for space needs |
| | 2. Determine if space is already available on campus | Fiscal Year 1 | This includes looking for possible reassignment of space but should be done with the least disruption possible |
| | 3. Review the institution's strategic and master building plans | Fiscal Years 1–2 | In this step, the goal is to assess the appropriateness of the new or renovated spaces and objectives with those of the strategic and master building plans |
| Feasibility and Approval | 4. Determine if the proposed projects are feasible | Fiscal Years 2–3 | This component should examine the need for space as related to other requests and rationales for additional or new space as well as necessary time commitments if the project is undertaken |
| | 5. Get the right approvals (different for public and private institutions) | Fiscal Year 2 | For public institutions, it is likely that more than the board will have input into the process, and more importantly, state laws may require additional approvals beyond those of the board. For private institutions, this part of the process is often easier |
| Build or Acquire | 6. Make the purchase or build the space | Fiscal Years 3–4 | Once the preceding steps have been taken, it is then time to either build the space or purchase the item. Though this seems relatively straightforward, it may take many years and involve budget complications |

*Source:* Adapted from Goldstein's (2012) list.

as external variables fluctuate. In a related vein, the costs of depreciation are dealt with on the operating side.

Third and finally, if the institution chooses to employ debt, there is the matter of debt service. The costs of paying back the debt plus interest are decidedly part of the operating budget. All of these considerations are part of prudent fiscal administration and should be part of capital budgeting decisions.

Now that readers are a bit more familiar with the process of capital budgeting, the next step is to understand how institutions can go about financing large projects or acquisitions. As there are a number of possible alternatives for acquiring capital assets, the focus is on those not needing debt in this chapter. Again, this does not necessarily change the decision-making process in terms of the final choice of acquisition, but it can certainly impact the fiscal sustainability and positioning of the institution.

## FUNDING NEW PROJECTS WITHOUT DEBT

In higher education there are a number of ways to pay for capital investments that do not require the issuance of debt. Though in recent years the tendency of institutions to employ debt for capital projects has been on the rise (Jacob, Stange, & McCall, 2013; Serna, 2013b, c), we, nonetheless, wish to highlight the funding mechanisms available to colleges and universities seeking to undertake or acquire capital projects and assets. We not only wish to highlight those alternatives available to institutions, but also illustrate some of their limitations. Let us begin with capital fund-raising or capital campaigns.

### Capital Fund-Raising and Campaigns

Capital fund-raising and campaigns are examples of what Barr and McClellan (2011) call "focused giving." This type of fund-raising is directed at a specific project deemed of importance either in the institution's master building plan or strategic plan. While fund-raising has certainly been part of the higher education landscape for some time, the character of capital campaigns has shifted. Previously, capital campaigns focused on raising funds for buildings or renovations.

Recently, however, they have focused more on program needs such as scholarships, endowed chairs, and fellowships than on physical plant needs (Barr & McClellan, 2011, p. 37). The reason a capital campaign is so attractive is that it has the added advantage of providing a large amount of funding for a project without requiring repayment or incurring debt costs. Moreover, this type of capital acquisition is relatively limited to higher education and other nonprofit areas (Finkler et al., 2013).

While capital campaigns have some very attractive attributes, they also come with some significant limitations. First, this type of fund-raising is restricted only to the project for which it is raised. In other words, if the project is not undertaken or ends with a surplus of funds, these monies cannot be shifted to another budgeting category or priority (Finkler et al., 2013). Second, development offices might find that donors are less willing or able to donate to other important areas. For example, an important part of fund-raising is for the development of scholarships and permanent additions to endowments.

If donors make gifts to an institution during a capital campaign, the institution is implicitly making a tradeoff that affects other long-term budget areas and priorities. Third, raising money for a capital acquisition that is a campus priority can take a great deal of time and energy. It is not unusual for capital campaigns to last many years before raising the needed funds. As institutions determine the capital needs, this should be part of the deliberation process. That is to say, if the capital needs of the institution are urgent, a capital campaign may not be the most expeditious way to raise funds.

## Paygo and Usage of Fund Balances

Paygo is a system of capital budgeting that pays for capital projects out of currently available funds rather than issuing long-term debt. As with other approaches that do not employ debt, it is attractive because the institution does not have to pay interest costs. However, it does suffer from some rather important limitations.

While useful for smaller institutions, the primary limitation of this approach is that it requires significant forethought around capital acquisitions and future needs. This approach requires that yearly capital expenditures remain fairly even from year to year (Lee, Johnson, & Joyce, 2013). If an institution can sufficiently forecast needed capital acquisitions and set aside monies from current funds to cover these expenditures, then Paygo is a viable approach.

However, most institutions of higher education require large, variable, less predictable amounts of capital financing. This suggests that Paygo is likely more applicable to smaller capital acquisitions than larger projects and is better suited to smaller institutions (Lee et al., 2013). Another significant limitation of this approach is that it requires that monies from current funding sources are used to finance capital projects.

This means that institutions are required to make a tradeoff regarding current spending and long-term benefits. In other words, institutions may have to spend less on other important operating functions in order to maintain a capital budget in this manner. Moreover, Paygo is particularly difficult to maintain if economic conditions worsen or unexpected fluctuations in antici-pated revenues or expenditures arise. When fiscal conditions are volatile, capital budgets using Paygo may simply be sacrificed to make up for short-falls occurring in other parts of the budget (Lee et al., 2013).

Similar to Paygo, the usage of fund balances relies on current funds. The difference, however, is that it relies on excess funds from the operating bud-get after accounting for all liabilities and assets (Governmental Accounting Standards Board, 2006). Assuming that these funds are not restricted, they can be employed to fund capital projects or acquisitions. However, the use of this funding source suffers from the same limitations outlined for Paygo approaches. Finally, and distinct from the Paygo approach, is that while Paygo deliberately sets aside funds for capital projects, the use of fund bal-ances relies on monies that are left over from operating expenses and rev-enues, thereby making them less stable from year to year.

## TIME VALUE OF MONEY

In the process of capital budgeting, time plays an important role for decision-making. This is because the value of money in the future is not the same as money in the present and vice versa. To put it differently, just like $100 today is not the same as $100 fifty years ago, $100 today is not worth the same amount as $100 fifty years from today. The reason for this is that the further away the acquisition of a dollar amount is from the present the less it is worth in the present and the longer an investment sits accruing interest the larger the amount will be.

As noted before, the true fiscal impact of a capital project or acquisition can be understood only in terms of its useful life. As this is the case, the TVM plays an important role in determining how capital funds will be allocated, and also which projects provide the most benefits for the costs. This section summarizes some basic concepts related to the TVM and includes some examples of how it is used in practice.

### Discounting and Compounding Basics

This section presents the basic method for determining the present (dis-counted) and future (compounded) values of money. To start, let us examine how discounting works to provide us a proper valuation technique for making decisions about the present dollar value of some amount in the future. Follow-ing Dunn (2012, pp. 229–33) and Finkler et al. (2013, pp. 167–71), one would employ the following equation to determine the present discounted value of monies stated in future terms:

$$PV = \frac{FV}{(1+i)^N}.$$

In order to employ this equation correctly, a few pieces of information are required. First, let us assume that the institution has decided that it will enhance student services by providing extra tutoring space on campus. It is able to spend $25,000 on the space today (an outlay) and will receive this money back in three years from some external source. However, this budgeting decision does not account for the difference in time between the outlay and the recouping of costs. In order for the transaction to make sense, the fiscal manager must account for time in the decision-making process. To do so requires the use of the equation presented earlier.

To make this more concrete, assume that the total number of discount periods[1] away from the present is equal to three. Also, assume that the going market rate for borrowing is 5%. With this information, we have enough data to determine how much $25,000 would be worth in today's dollars. If we insert these values into the *PV* equation, we get:

$$PV = \frac{\$25,000}{(1+.05)^3} \ or \approx \$21,596.$$

Hence, this equation indicates that the present discounted value of $25,000 received three years from now would actually cover only $21,596 of the project. Another way to approach this is from calculating the discount factor (*DF*) using the approach laid out by Dunn (2012, p. 231):

$$DF = \frac{1}{(1+r)^n}.$$

This is done with an equation that provides us with a factor for discounting any amount using information about the market interest rate (*r*) and number of periods (*n*) for which the values must be discounted or compounded. For this example, this would look like:

$$DF = \frac{1}{(1+.05)^3} \ or \approx .8638.$$

Doing so would allow the budget manager to use this discount rate for any value, not just the $25,000 in our example, with close approximation. Say, for example, that a capital project requires an outlay of $150,000, and the market rate, as well as the number of periods, remains the same. Using the discount factor, this calculation is simple:

$$\$150,000 \times .8638 = \$129,570.$$

It is also very close to the value obtained from the *PV* equation above ($129,575.64).

If the fiscal manager had some leeway to negotiate for the full amount required to cover the total cost of the tutoring services, then this requires the use of the following equation for the calculation of future compounded value.

$$FV = PV(1+i)^N.$$

So in a similar fashion, this requires the same information as the *PV* equation. To do so, insert the needed values into the equation to come up with:

$$FV = 25,000(1+.05)^3 \ or \approx \$28,941.$$

This indicates that in order to fully cover the costs of this capital outlay, one would require $28,941 in three years as opposed to $25,000.

The reason for this larger value is that it is assumed that money today could be invested at the market rate and because of compounding—earning interest on interest earned—can grow more quickly. This basic assumption is what accounts for the difference in the terms of *PV* as compared to *FV*. Another important consideration for *FV*, or compounding, is that interest may not be paid on a yearly basis. In fact, many investments pay biannually or quarterly.

To illustrate, suppose that the institution has decided it will undertake the tutoring services project on in three years and has $25,000 today that it can invest today to pay for the project.[2] Based on the earlier example it is clear that with interest and compounding paid yearly this would result in a return of $28,941. But what happens if interest is not compounded annually but instead is compounded twice a year? This requires a reworking of the *FV* equation to reflect this fact.

The *FV* equation's interest rate has to be divided by the number of compound periods in a year and the number of periods increased. In this case, the total number of periods would rise from three to six and the interest rate would go from 5% to 2.5%. This is necessary because of the way in which compounding works, namely, that the investment earns interest upon interest earned in previous periods.[3] Since the needed information is available, the next step is simply to plug in the new values into the *FV* equation:

$$FV = 25,000(1+.025)^6 \ or \approx \$28,992.$$

This example shows the power of compounding in that the value over the same three-year period is increased slightly thanks to interest payments happening twice a year. If the same example were used with quarterly payments, the total amount in three years would total approximately $29,019. While these values may not seem very different, as both the number of interest payments per year and the number of years increase, this can have a very large impact on the *FV* of an amount invested today.

This section has outlined the basic mechanics of discounting and compounding. However, in day-to-day fiscal administration, it is not often the case that outlays and investments work out so smoothly. In the next section, some foundations of cost–benefit analysis as related to the TVM are presented. Also included is the concept of net present value (NPV) and benefit/revenue streams and their relationship to decision-making as well as the compounding and discounting.

As a final note in this section, the importance of time and periods in the calculation of *PV* and *FV* warrants mention. For both, as the calculation takes into account periods further and further in the future, the accuracy of estimates becomes more volatile and as a result less precise. This has to do with normal business cycles and market fluctuations. It is also related to the fact that discount rates are unlikely to remain constant over many years or periods. Discount rates are better understood as a reflection of human assumptions about market behavior and activity.

Hence, as fiscal administrators in higher education account for time, they must also be careful not to make assumptions in their calculations of *PV* and *FV* that are too stringent or not based in the reality of economic activity. Making assumptions that discount rates will remain high or low can result in *PV*s and *FV*s that are off by a considerable amount. Still, as long as prudent measures are taken, multiple scenarios considered, and assumptions clearly and carefully laid out, the calculation of both many years into the future can provide useful information for decision-making in the present.

## ANNUAL CASH FLOWS AND CHOOSING PROJECTS

The previously outlined models used in TVM calculations provide a fundamental process for making correct comparisons when outlays are required and/or investments are paid back at some single point in time. The limitation with these techniques, however, is that they do not allow for the inclusion of either annual payments or costs associated with a project. A way to get around this limitation is to include these cash flows as part of the analysis.

As a departure from previous chapters and sections, this chapter employs a number of Excel screenshots given that the process for calculating many of the values in the next few sections is quite cumbersome when done using mathematical approaches that use formulas requiring yearly calculations. In any event, the formulas employed in this section are applicable to the *FV* and *PV* examples provided earlier, with the simple exclusion of the [pmt] portion of the Excel formula function.

## Future Value with Annuities

Sometimes institutions are able to set aside funds for some future project and may also find themselves in a position where it is possible to add to the initial investment. To illustrate, suppose that a college or university wishes to replace computers in a small department in the near future at what they expect to be just over $30,000. They know that the department does not have sufficient funds to do so today, and they also know that the current systems will remain adequate for the next three years.

In this case, assume that the institution wishes to know how much $25,000 will be worth in three years if invested at 5%, but it is also known that the department can add an additional $1,000 per year to the initial investment. Essentially, the institution is able to invest the principal but is also able to add to the principal amount during the investment period. Hence, if the principal is only invested, then the *FV* of the $25,000 would simply take on the values calculated previously in this chapter and would total approximately $28,941 if interest was compounded once a year.

With this in mind, however, it is possible to calculate what the *FV* of the principal plus additional monies would equal at the end of three years by using a modified *FV* equation. As this formula becomes very cumbersome quickly, it is best presented as an Excel spreadsheet equation as in the screenshots in Figure 8.1.

| MEDIAN | ▼ | × ✓ *fx* | =FV( |
|---|---|---|---|
|  | A | B | C | D |
| 1 |  |  |  |  |
| 2 | Rate | 5% |  |  |
| 3 | Periods | 3 |  |  |
| 4 | Payment | (1000) |  |  |
| 5 | PV= | (25000) |  |  |
| 6 | =FV( |  |  |  |
| 7 | FV(rate, nper, pmt, [pv], [type]) |  |  |  |
| 8 |  |  |  |  |

**Figure 8.1   Excel Example 1.** *Source:* Example adapted and expanded from Finkler et al., 2013.

The Excel formula for *FV* provides a space for all of the information necessary for this calculation.

In Figure 8.2, values are plugged in for each required variable except [type]. A few notes about employing this formula in Excel are required before proceeding. First, when using the *FV* functionality in Excel, it is possible to simply click on the cell (use cell references) to fill in the formula. The result would be as shown in Figure 8.3.

Regardless of how one chooses to input the information the final calculation should equal $32,093.13 as in Figure 8.4. Readers will notice that both the payment (pmt) and *PV* values are included as negative values. This is primarily for reporting given that the goal is always to report the estimated value as a positive. Hence, both of these values must be entered as negatives. Also, comma separators for monetary values in Excel were not included.

| MEDIAN | ▾ | × ✓ *fx* | =FV(.05, 3, -1000, -25000) | | |
|---|---|---|---|---|---|
| | A | B | C | D | E | F |
| 1 | | | | | | |
| 2 | Rate | 5% | | | | |
| 3 | Periods | 3 | | | | |
| 4 | Payment | (1000) | | | | |
| 5 | PV= | (25000) | | | | |
| 6 | =FV(.05, 3, -1000, -25000) | | | | | |

**Figure 8.2  Excel Example 2.** *Source*: Examples adapted and expanded from Finkler et al., 2013.

| MEDIAN | ▾ | × ✓ *fx* | =FV(B2,B3,B4,B5) | |
|---|---|---|---|---|
| | A | B | C | D | E |
| 1 | | | | | |
| 2 | Rate | 5% | | | |
| 3 | Periods | 3 | | | |
| 4 | Payment | (1000) | | | |
| 5 | PV= | (25000) | | | |
| 6 | =FV(B2,B3,B4,B5) | | | | |
| 7 | FV(rate, nper, pmt, [pv], [type]) | | | | |
| 8 | | | | | |

**Figure 8.3  Excel Example 3.** *Source*: Example adapted and expanded from Finkler et al., 2013.

This is because commas are used to separate the different variables from one another. So if one were to include 1,000, then Excel would read this as a payment equal to one, and a *PV* equal to 000.

Finally, it was noted earlier that a value for [type] was not included in the equation. This value is included as a way to indicate to Excel whether payments are happening at the beginning or end of a year and Excel automatically defaults to 0 assuming an end-of-the-year payment. For example, the values for this illustration would change slightly if [type] was changed to equal 1 as in Figure 8.5.

| | A | B | C |
|---|---|---|---|
| 1 | | | |
| 2 | Rate | 5% | |
| 3 | Periods | 3 | |
| 4 | Payment | (1000) | |
| 5 | PV= | (25000) | |
| 6 | $32,093.13 | | |

*Cell reference: A7*

**Figure 8.4   Excel Example 4.** *Source*: Example adapted and expanded from Finkler et al., 2013.

| | A | B | C | D | E | F |
|---|---|---|---|---|---|---|
| 1 | | | | | | |
| 2 | Rate | 5% | | | | |
| 3 | Periods | 3 | | | | |
| 4 | Payment | (1000) | | | | |
| 5 | PV= | (25000) | | | | |
| 6 | =FV(0.05, 3, -1000, -25000, 1) | | | | | |
| 7 | FV(rate, nper, pmt, [pv], [type]) | | | | | |

*Formula bar (MEDIAN):* =FV(0.05, 3, -1000, -25000, 1)

**Figure 8.5   Excel Example 5.** *Source*: Example adapted and expanded from Finkler et al., 2013.

The *FV* with this inclusion is equal to $32,250.75 or slightly higher since monies added at the beginning of the year have more time to compound. Hence, the department, through investing $25,000 and adding $1,000 for three years, which would have totaled only $28,000 if not invested, now has more than sufficient funds to cover the costs of the new system. Finally, it is important to note that as earlier a reworking of the *FV* equation results in a useful *PV* equation that is applied to compare net present costs (NPCs) as well.

## Present Values with Annual Costs

Instead of having the luxury of setting aside monies for a few years to cover the costs of some new project, it is more often the case that fiscal managers must choose between two projects with different costs in the present. Fiscal manager are often asked to evaluate the NPC of multiple possibilities to determine which makes the most budgetary sense. To do so requires using the *PV* equation presented earlier in this chapter. Again, because this equation can become unwieldy quite quickly when including cash flows, it is presented here using Excel screenshots in a simplified version.

For this example, assume that the institution has to choose between two types of computers: Computer A and Computer B. Following Finkler et al.'s (2013, p. 176) example, the information is represented in Table 8.2.

From Table 8.2, it looks pretty obvious that Computer B has a higher total cost, and since most institutions seek out ways to cut costs, it might seem like a no-brainer to go with Computer A. However, this comparison is faulty. Before making a comparison, it is necessary to understand what is known about both computer options. It is clear that the initial outlay for Computer A is higher than that for Computer B, but the yearly costs for Computer A are substantially lower than for Computer B. With this in mind, we can now employ *PV* calculations to help make the comparison appropriate.

Using the *PV* formula available in Excel, it is simple enough to carry out the calculation of multiple years of costs assuming an interest rate of 5% and five years of associated annual costs[4] as shown in Figure 8.6. It is necessary

Table 8.2   Contrasting Computer Costs

|  | Computer A | Computer B |
| --- | --- | --- |
| Initial outlay | 7,500 | 4,350 |
| Yearly cost | 600 | 1,250 |
| Number of years | 5 | 5 |
| Total cost | 10,500 | 10,600 |

*Source*: Examples adapted from Finkler et al. (2013).

to calculate the *PV* of cash flows for each possible project. Again, readers will note that only the first three values are used in this instance and both [*fv*] and [type] are left out since this information is unavailable to us.

The results of these calculations are presented in Table 8.3. In this table, the cash flows for each project have been discounted. Now it is possible to make the appropriate comparisons by adding the initial outlay to these two values to obtain the NPC of each. Hence, Computer A's NPC is equal to the initial outlay or $7,500 plus $2,597.69 or $10,097.69. For Computer B, the total NPC is equal to $4,350 plus $5,411.85 or $9,761.85. This is presented in Table 8.4.

Hence, it is clear that in discounted terms, and taking into account the yearly costs associated with each type of computer, Computer B is actually the best option based on NPC; though if there are other considerations that are not financial, this still provides an appropriate comparison of costs when examining options.

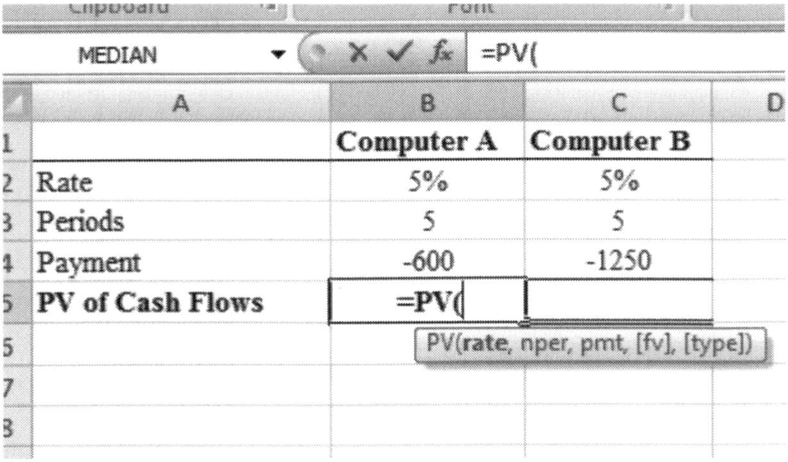

**Figure 8.6  Excel Example 6.** *Source*: Example adapted and expanded from Finkler et al., 2013.

**Table 8.3  Cash Flow Discounting for Each Project**

|  | Computer A | Computer B |
|---|---|---|
| Rate | 5% | 5% |
| Periods | 5 | 5 |
| Payment | 600 | 1,250 |
| PV of cash flows | 2,597.69 | 5,411.85 |

*Source*: Examples adapted from Finkler et al. (2014).

Table 8.4  Final Cost Comparisons Using NPC

|  | Computer A | Computer B |
|---|---|---|
| Initial outlay | 7,500 | 4,350 |
| PV cash flows | 2,597.69 | 5,411.85 |
| *Total NPC* | *10,097.69* | *9,761.85* |

Source: Examples adapted from Finkler et al. (2015).

With the help of this short illustration, it is our hope that readers are now familiar with the important role played by costs in the decision-making process. In the next section, we consider how projects are chosen based on situations where there are both costs and revenues associated with choosing a project that requires discounting.

## Net Present Value and Cash Flows

In this section, the foundational elements[5] associated with choosing capital projects that are associated with yearly costs and revenues are presented. As noted by Finkler et al. (2013, p. 180), the methods presented previously do not account for projects that impact both revenues and costs yearly. As this affects project valuation by requiring that the analysis account for annual cash flows, the NPV is a powerful device in the budget manager's toolkit. Now it is important to underscore that there are at least two ways to employ this technique that allow for different values of both cash inflows and outflows for every year.

To start, let us assume that the institution decided to go with Computer B from the previous example. While the NPC allows for estimating costs, it does not account for possible revenues that might accrue from choosing project B. For the sake of exposition, suppose that Computer B's system was able to be used by another institution in the evenings and as a result would generate a revenue stream over the useful life of five years. Additionally, to make things a bit more interesting, the example adjusts the yearly outflows or costs from the previous example so they are lumpier rather than the same year to year. Again, following Finkler et al. (2013, p. 181), we present Figure 8.7, which shows the screenshot of the setup for calculating the NPV.

In the screenshot, the goal was to make the calculation as simple as possible using Excel's cell reference and drag functionalities. From Figure 8.7 it is clear that the rate would stay the same over every year, that the payment would be equal to zero because we are taking each year on its own, and that period is related to number of years away from the current year where the outlay is $4,350 to acquire Computer B. Once we have calculated the net cash flow for each year, discounting is required for each cash flow. This is done using the very same method as earlier but for each year.

Figure 8.8 shows, with highlighting, how to go about calculating the *PV* for individual years using the cell reference function, and then simply dragging it across the row to obtain values for each year. If the setup is not exactly as in the figure, then caution must be exercised when clicking and calculating each year's PV. In order to calculate the value of interest to us, the NPV, one simply tells Excel that the wish is to sum all of the value in row 11 as in Figure 8.9.

From Figure 8.9, in cell B13, which is highlighted along with the function command, one simply tells Excel to sum cells B11 through G11, which automatically adds up all of the yearly *PV*s and subtracts initial outlay to give the NPV. For decision-making, if the NPV is negative and the decision to undertake a particular course of action is purely financial, then all projects with

| C13 | ▼ | $f_x$ | | | | |
|---|---|---|---|---|---|---|
| | A | B | C | D | E | F | G |
| 1 | | | | | | | |
| 2 | Rate | 5% | 5% | 5% | 5% | 5% | 5% |
| 3 | Payment | 0 | 0 | 0 | 0 | 0 | 0 |
| 4 | Period | 0 | 1 | 2 | 3 | 4 | 5 |
| 5 | | | | | | | |
| 6 | | Year 0 | Year 1 | Year 2 | Year 3 | Year 4 | Year 5 |
| 7 | Cash In Flow | 0 | 1200 | 1200 | 1250 | 1400 | 1475 |
| 8 | Cash Out Flow | -4350 | -800 | -1025 | -1375 | -1450 | -1600 |
| 9 | Net Cash Flow | -4350 | 400 | 175 | -125 | -50 | -125 |
| 10 | | | | | | | |

**Figure 8.7   Excel Example 7.** *Source*: Example adapted and expanded from Finkler et al., 2013.

| C11 | ▼ | $f_x$ | =PV(B2, C4, B3, -C9) | | | |
|---|---|---|---|---|---|---|
| | A | B | C | D | E | F | G |
| 1 | | | | | | | |
| 2 | Rate | 5% | 5% | 5% | 5% | 5% | 5% |
| 3 | Payment | 0 | 0 | 0 | 0 | 0 | 0 |
| 4 | Period | 0 | 1 | 2 | 3 | 4 | 5 |
| 5 | | | | | | | |
| 6 | | Year 0 | Year 1 | Year 2 | Year 3 | Year 4 | Year 5 |
| 7 | Cash In Flow | 0 | 1200 | 1200 | 1250 | 1400 | 1475 |
| 8 | Cash Out Flow | -4350 | -800 | -1025 | -1375 | -1450 | -1600 |
| 9 | Net Cash Flow | -4350 | 400 | 175 | -125 | -50 | -125 |
| 10 | | | | | | | |
| 11 | Present Value of Individual Cash Flows | -4350 | $380.95 | $158.73 | ($107.98) | ($41.14) | ($97.94) |
| 12 | | | | | | | |
| 13 | Net Present Value | -4057.37 | | | | | |

**Figure 8.8   Excel Example 8.** *Source*: Example adapted and expanded from Finkler et al., 2013.

| B13 | | $f_x$ =SUM(B11:G11) | | | | |
|---|---|---|---|---|---|---|
| A | B | C | D | E | F | G |
| 1 | | | | | | |
| 2 Rate | 5% | 5% | 5% | 5% | 5% | 5% |
| 3 Payment | 0 | 0 | 0 | 0 | 0 | 0 |
| 4 Period | 0 | 1 | 2 | 3 | 4 | 5 |
| 5 | | | | | | |
| 6 | Year 0 | Year 1 | Year 2 | Year 3 | Year 4 | Year 5 |
| 7 Cash In Flow | 0 | 1200 | 1200 | 1250 | 1400 | 1475 |
| 8 Cash Out Flow | -4350 | -800 | -1025 | -1375 | -1450 | -1600 |
| 9 Net Cash Flow | -4350 | 400 | 175 | -125 | -50 | -125 |
| 10 | | | | | | |
| 11 Present Value of Individual Cash Flows | -4350 | $380.95 | $158.73 | ($107.98) | ($41.14) | ($97.94) |
| 12 | | | | | | |
| 13 Net Present Value | -4057.37 | | | | | |

Figure 8.9 Excel Example 9. *Source*: Example adapted and expanded from Finkler et al., 2013.

negative NPVs should be rejected. However, if the decision is not based only on NPVs but other contextual factors, this comparison, like the NPC, provides valuable information about the financial portion of the decision and whether it falls short or provides a positive cash flow stream (Finkler et al., 2013).

## CHOOSING THE DISCOUNT RATE

For budget managers, many decisions are focused on their impact on today's bottom line. Hence, there is a strong focus on choosing how to report and relate future dollars in today's monetary values. In the examples provided in this chapter, we have simply assumed that the discount rate was a given. This is problematic for fiscal administration on the whole because choosing a rate is fraught with many dilemmas.

A primary concern when accounting for the TVM is choosing a rate that best reflects the conditions facing the institution or the economy as a whole. Because the discount rate is often considered the hurdle rate, or the rate required to break-even on a capital project, it must be closely tied to institution's costs of capital (Finkler et al., 2013). Moreover, if the fiscal environment is volatile, a conservative move to deal with this uncertainty is to increase the discount rate.

Still, this is extremely difficult to do well, and as a result there are often many ways to choose the discount rate. As noted by Finkler et al. (2013, p. 185), "In practice, there is little consistency in the discount rate used across government even within branches of the same government," and the same likely holds for institutions of higher education as well.

Nonetheless, Dunn (2012, pp. 232–33) provides some guidance around choosing a discount rate for public-sector entities. These include:

- Private-sector rates—These rates are based on the going interest rates in private markets with the assumption that tax monies could have been invested at these rates. The limitation with this approach is that it does not reflect external social costs and is a better indication of individual or narrow group preferences.
- Social rates—These rates are based on the social time preference related to the collective value of some cost or benefit realized into the future; it is especially concerned with the welfare of future generations. It attempts to overcome the short-term emphasis often placed on TVM analysis. Still, it is often accused of being inefficient because it is lower than private rates.
- Government rates—These rates are based on the current costs of borrowing faced by governments. The difficulty in using this rate is that different levels of government often borrow at different rates. Additionally, it does not account for the opportunity cost associated when monies are not invested.

As is evident, each one of these alternatives has both advantages and limitations. In any event, the goal should be to incorporate as much information about the fiscal environment as possible as budget managers undertake the analysis of investments in capital projects and their true costs.

Finally, there exists some concern around choosing a discount rate while accounting for inflationary pressures. A preferred approach is to forecast anticipated inflationary pressures on inflows and outflows before calculating the *PV* and *FV* of each. Another approach is to include the anticipated inflation rate in the discount rate. The limitation introduced with this approach is that it does not account for differences in the impacts of inflationary pressures on different inflows or outflows.


## CONCLUSION

This chapter has provided a basic overview of the capital budgeting process and cycle. It has included a basic introduction to the importance of the TVM and its related concepts such as future value, present value, annuities, NPC, and NPV. Additionally, it has provided guidance for the choosing of projects and a discount rate in the capital budgeting process. While the emphasis in this chapter has been on capital budgeting without debt, the same concepts apply to the capital budgeting cycle and process with debt. In the next chapter, this is examined further.

## QUESTIONS AND EXERCISES FOR CAPITAL BUDGETING WITHOUT DEBT

1. How does capital budgeting differ from operational budgeting?
2. What are the major approaches to capital budgeting when trying to avoid the use of debt?
3. How is capital budgeting related to operational budgeting?
4. Why does there exist a need to take into consideration how money changes value over time? How does this relate to fiscal administration and budgeting decisions?
5. Using the following vignettes, employ the *discounting* techniques presented in this chapter:
   a. Assume that the institution has a capital asset that will be worth $99,523.03 in five years and that the discount rate for this time period is 3%. Provide the present value of this capital asset. What happens to the value of this asset if the discount rate changes to 5%? Compare how the change in discount rates affects the assumed value of the asset.
   b. Assume that the institution has a capital asset that will be worth $93,862.47 in ten years and that the discount rate for this time period is 3%. Provide the present value of this capital asset. What happens to the value of this asset if the discount rate changes to 3.5%? Compare how the change in discount rates affects the assumed value of the asset.
   c. Assume that the institution has a capital asset that will be worth $120,844 in twenty years and that the discount rate for this time period is 3%. Provide the present value of this capital asset. What happens if the discount rate changes to 4%? Compare how the change in discount rates affects the assumed value of the asset.
6. What happens to the confidence of the estimated value of our asset as we go further into the future assuming a particular discount rate?
7. After completing the previous three exercises, comment on how accurate each is likely to be based on the specifics of each problem. Is a five-, ten-, or twenty-year forecast more accurate? Explain why each is or isn't more accurate? What should a fiscal manager consider when calculating *PVs* using a twenty-year period?
8. Which factors should be included when choosing a discount rate? How should capital budgeting incorporate inflationary concerns?
9. Using the following vignettes, employ the *compounding* techniques presented in this chapter:
   a. Assume that an institution will invest $117,315.40 for five years and that the discount rate for this time period is 5%. Provide the future

value of this investment. What happens to the value of this investment if the interest (discount) rate changes to 3%? Compare how the change in rates affects the assumed value of the investment.

b. Assume that an institution will invest $109,633.30 for ten years and that the discount rate for this time period is 5%. Provide the future value of this investment. What happens to the value of this investment if the interest rate changes to 3%? Compare how the change in rates affects the assumed value of the investment.

c. Assume that an institution will invest $95,876.21 for twenty years and that the discount rate for this time period is 5%. Provide the future value of this investment. What happens to the value of this investment if the interest rate changes to 3%? Compare how the change in rates affects the assumed value of the investment.

d. Using the information from Exercise c, reexamine this problem, but this time, assume that compounding happens twice a year. Compare the differences in the investment value at 5% and at 3% to those calculated in Exercise c. How does this change the calculation? What happens to the value of an investment when compound periods are increased to more than once a year?

10. Using the information provided, as well as Microsoft Excel, use the ideas presented around *cash flows and decision-making* to answer the following questions:

An institution must choose between providing an art exhibition space with the following outlays and cash flows. Using examples provided in this chapter, calculate the NPC for each project and explain which exhibition space should be chosen based solely on the NPC.

11. Briefly describe how the process would be different for calculating the NPC if the cash flows differed from time period to time period?

12. Should the NPC be the most important or only determinant for choosing a project? If so, why? If not, what others things might be included?

**Table 8.5   NPC Exercise**

|                  | Exhibition A | Exhibition B |
|------------------|:------------:|:------------:|
| Initial outlay   | 10,500       | 6,350        |
| Yearly cost      | 500          | 1,200        |
| Periods (years)  | 5            | 5            |
| Interest rate    | 4.5%         | 4.5%         |
| Total cost       | *13,000*     | *12,350*     |

*Source*: Examples adapted from Finkler et al. (2016).

# NOTES

1. For ease of analysis, in the instance, periods are understood as years because the market rate of interest is assumed to be paid annually. However, this can change even for compounding periods presented in this chapter.

2. Based on the *PV* example presented earlier, it is clear that the institution needs to invest about $21,596 today at 5% to receive $25,000 in three years.

3. If the *FV* is already known, another possibility is to discount the *FV* by the increased number of periods and lower rate when interest is paid more than once a year to obtain the needed amount for investment today or the *PV*.

4. It is possible to assume that yearly payments are not equal over time, however, that is beyond the scope of the current text. See Finkler et al. (2013) for more on this.

5. For detailed explanation and treatment of valuation, cash flow, and discount models, see Damodaran (2001, 2012).

*Chapter 9*

# Capital Budgeting and Debt

Institutions of higher education often face capital budgeting choices that require more funds than the institution has readily available either in reserves or as surpluses to the operating budget. This requires that colleges and universities employ debt to carry out these projects. To help those individuals new to the fiscal administration of higher education, this chapter provides a brief introduction and overview to capital budgeting as related to issuing and using debt as a financing tool.

As the foundations of fiscal analysis regarding the time value of money do not change for the issuance of bonds, the fundamentals covered in chapter 8 remain largely unchanged for capital budgeting with this type of debt and hence are not covered here. Also, the intricacies of bond issuance and debt management are beyond the scope of the current text; however, those wishing to obtain a more nuanced and accessible understanding of the process should see Doty (2012), Mincke (2008), and O'Hara (2012).

## WHY USE DEBT?

Generally speaking, colleges and universities will issue debt in the form of bonds to finance large capital projects. Examples of these projects include the construction, refurbishment, or renovation of libraries, academic buildings, administrative buildings, sports facilities, and so on (Mincke, 2008). Additionally, and as noted in chapter 8, the capital budgeting process takes place over a number of years and is decidedly related to the long-term goals of the institution (Barr & McClellan, 2011; Goldstein, 2012).

As a result, projects requiring debt financing should include both long- and short-term considerations since servicing this debt typically requires long-standing dedication of financial resources both in the form of debt-service and operating and maintenance expenses. Moreover, although some of the financing methods mentioned previously such as Paygo and capital campaigns offer the prospect of funding these projects without debt or interest costs (Lee Jr., Johnson, & Joyce, 2013), they are often limited to short-term fund-raising capacities.

Therefore, issuing bonds to finance a project serves institutional goals in at least two ways. First, it allows the institution to fund projects that would be outside the scope of their operating finances. Issuing debt in the form of bonds provides a mechanism for "leveraging" the institution's assets. In other words, it allows the institution to acquire capital assets that will help it fulfill its mission, goals, and vision by using debt to build, renovate, refurbish, or purchase land without putting undue strain on operating budgets, waiting to build up reserves, or undertaking a capital campaign.

Second, it allows the institution to spread the costs of a large capital acquisition or project over a much longer period of time. Debt service and depreciation of capital assets are spread over the useful life of a project. This means that the institution reports only the depreciation and debt service for the current fiscal year. Additionally, using long-term debt financing provides a mechanism for having future groups of students, who will derive the majority of benefits from the project, bear some of the responsibility for funding it.

Finally, a central concern in bond issuance has to do with how a project is secured. That is to say, an institution must determine which assets or revenue streams it will pledge to finance the project. This is where it is necessary to distinguish between *general obligation bonds* and *revenue bonds*. General obligation bonds, or GO for short, are bonds that are backed by the full faith and credit of the issuing body. For higher education institutions, this typically means that the payment for bonds is secured by tuition and fee, state funding, and grant and contract revenues.

In the case of revenue bonds, these are backed only by the revenues related to the project or a specific source. Examples of this include student housing or sports facilities (Finkler et al., 2013; Mincke, 2008) where the revenues generated by the project go to servicing the debt. Revenue bonds are often issued by what would be considered auxiliary units of the university, including housing, parking, and medical centers, and for the most part will charge user fees to help service debt.

## CREDIT RATINGS AND FACTORS RELATED TO BOND RATES

In determining how much an institution will pay for debt, credit ratings agencies consider a number of factors in order to rate colleges and universities.[1]

This rating offers information for those who purchase bonds and provides a means of establishing default risk associated with a specific institution. Because ratings include a great deal of both contextual and financial information, they provide a quick metric for bond-buyers regarding how likely an institution is to default on the debt principal and it associated interest costs (Serna, 2013a, b).

## Credit Rating Symbols and Qualifiers

Before detailing the importance of ratings to capital budgeting, the goal is to first examine credit ratings and the symbols associated with them. Table 9.1 details each credit rating and includes information on indicators that serve as qualifiers or grades to signify an institution's relative standing within each of the categories. A quick note: Table 9.1 includes only those ratings issued by Standard & Poor's (S&P) and Moody's given their long history rating colleges and universities.[2]

Generally speaking, educational organizations, and institutions of higher education in particular, enjoy relatively high, stable credit ratings. However, this trend has changed recently with downgrades becoming more commonplace (Bogaty & Nelson, 2013; Daley, 2010; Inside Higher Ed, 2013; S&P, 2013) due primarily to the economic downturn of 2008. When viewed in aggregate, the sector remains rather stable, though S&P (2013) noted that downgrades as compared to upgrades were increasing since at least 2008.

**Table 9.1   Credit Ratings for Nonprofit Colleges and Universities**

|  | *S&P* | *Moody's* |  |
| --- | --- | --- | --- |
| Highest rating | AAA | Aaa | Highest rating |
|  | AA | Aa |  |
|  | A | A |  |
|  | BBB | Baa |  |
| Speculative | BB | Ba | Speculative |
|  | B | B |  |
|  | CCC | Caa |  |
|  | CC | Ca |  |
|  | C | C | In default/lowest rating |
| In default/lowest rating* | D | N/A |  |
| Qualifiers | Plus and minus indicate a relatively stronger/weaker position in the category | 1 indicates a higher, 2 a median, and 3 a lower position in the category |  |

*Sources*: Serna (2013a, b), reproduced with permission.
*Note that in the case of the default credit rating S&P maintains one rating more than does Moody's.

Still, S&P notes that in 2012 only 10% of college and university credit ratings were considered to have an outlook rated as something other than "stable."

While the news from S&P is somewhat more positive than Moody's in terms of its general outlook for the sector, both agencies remain tentative regarding possible changes, for better or for worse, impacting credit ratings in higher education. While the vast majority of colleges and universities are seen as creditworthy, increasing levels of deferred maintenance and competitive pressures will undoubtedly require that institutions secure capital financing. For example, as of 2009, education alone made up over 22% of municipal bonds issues (O'Hara, 2012).

In bond markets, an institution's credit rating determines how much the institution will pay for this debt over the long run. The expenses associated with issuing bonds are directly related to the creditworthiness of the issuing entity. In other words, even for institutions within the same category, the costs associated with bond issuance can vary considerably based on differing qualifiers.

## Ratings, Debt Service, and the Operating Budget

The fact that ratings, and their accompanying qualifiers, determine interest costs on bond issues results in at least a few important considerations for budget and financial planners at colleges and universities. First, operating budgets must be able to accommodate debt-service and depreciation costs as well as those concomitant expenses required to bring and keep a project online.

Second, bond issues impact an institution's debt profile and total debt-burden. Once debt has been issued for a particular project, credit becomes unavailable for other projects. Again, this will impact long-run fiscal positioning because the pledge of operating revenues means that they cannot be pledged for other projects. Moreover, this could signal to debt markets that the institution has overleveraged its assets since increasing debt burden requires increasing pledges of institutional operating funds into the future.

Third, in the process of making decisions about the uses of limited resources, changes in an institution's credit rating could indicate that decision-makers are not making the best tradeoffs as far as debt markets are concerned. Indeed, a major part of the ratings process is related to how institutions employ and have employed debt in the past. Furthermore, rating agencies carefully examine current and previous debt-management and debt-service policies (Serna, 2013a, b).

Finally, although some colleges and universities have the ability to generate stronger than average demand, it is almost never the case that institutions can fund all priorities. In fact, S&P (2013) and Moody's (2013) both provide evidence that while tuition and fees have become the single largest budgetary component for the sector as a whole, private institutions are not faring as well as publics given their reliance on this revenue source. This is further developed in the next section, which briefly examines the factors associated with credit ratings that are both within and outside of an institution's control, but which nonetheless are part of the rating profile.

## Associated Rating Factors

Evaluating the creditworthiness of higher education institutions is fraught with many complexities. Rating agencies evaluate a vast array of institutional, state, and financial characteristics. Mostly, the agencies wish to establish institutional demand and market-positioning, finances and operating performance, internal and external management and governance. They also consider an institution's debt profile, state policies, and mandates, and the relationship maintained with state governing boards and other oversight bodies.

Table 9.2 outlines the general credit rating criteria, including some examples of how each category is evaluated. Based on the rather significant demands placed on institutions for determining creditworthiness, the information contained in a rating serves as an important indicator for institutional financial managers, debt markets, and often-external stakeholders. The rating supplies information on short- and long-run fiscal stability of an institution.

**Table 9.2   General Public Higher Education Credit Rating Criteria**

| Criteria | Measured via |
| --- | --- |
| Market position and demand | Enrollments, number of applications, number of students accepted, student quality, student yield, retention and graduation rates, percent of tenured faculty, and competition |
| Finances and operating performance | Revenues (including tuition and state appropriations), expenses, risk management, operating budgets and balance sheets, endowment and long-term investment pools, liquidity provisions, and total debt burden |
| Governance and management | Overall institutional strategies and policies implemented by university administration, track record of dealing with unforeseen difficulties, tenure of management, and composition and structure of the university governing board, reporting mechanisms and monitoring procedures |
| Debt profile | Security pledges, debt covenants, as well as other liabilities and debt instruments |
| State policies and government relationship | Mandated tuition-caps, declines in budgetary resources provided by the state, requiring remission of surpluses or unspent dollars back to the state, bonding limits, and relationship with the state board |

*Source*: Serna (2013b, c), reproduced with permission.

As a result, it often provides invaluable information and guidance for future strategic endeavors both internally and externally.

This section has sketched only a preview into what is generally a multifaceted practice for rating institutions. However, it is clear that the rating agencies evaluate colleges and universities based on a multitude of factors, some within the purview of institutional control and others less so. For example, many institutions do not have the authority to unilaterally issue debt (Barr & McClellan, 2011). In fact, for public institutions it is not uncommon to seek approval from the state before issuing debt or in the beginning of the capital budgeting process.

Finally, credit rating agencies have stated that a number of the factors they consider when rating institutions are difficult to quantify. Still, the highly contextual operational environment facing each institution remains exceedingly important for determining a credit rating and by extensions debt-costs. In order to understand the complexity of the process a bit better, the next section looks at how institutions go about issuing debt and the actors in the process.

## ACTORS IN THE BOND PROCESS AND STEPS FOR ISSUING DEBT

As can be inferred from the previous section, issuing debt is complicated. To help illuminate some of the components of a debt issue, this section provides a concise introduction to the process including some of the major actors. It then outlines the major steps associated with a bond issue that relate directly to higher education. Again, the goal here is to provide a 35,000-foot view of the process. Those seeking a more nuanced understanding should consult Feldstein and Fabozzi (2008) or O'Hara (2012).

### Actors in a Bond Issue

In most bond issues, actors can be broken up into three categories: the issuers, the bond dealers, and the investors. In the section that follows, each of these actors is discussed along with a brief description based on O'Hara (2012, pp. 4–22).

*Issuers*

The issuers in this instance are institutions of higher education (Ely 2012). For many public institutions, this might require state approval and for just about every institution, the Board of Trustees must approve bond issues.

Additionally, public institutions, along with their P-12 counterparts, may have access to statewide credit enhancement programs that serve as an alternative to traditional, private bond insurance (Ely, 2012), which is often used to help lower interest costs associated with a bond issue.

## Bond Dealers

This group usually includes public finance specialists, underwriters, traders, sales, research and credit analysts, operations, and bond counsel. Public finance specialists, who are investment bankers, serve as the point of contact for issuers and underwriters. They provide guidance for the sale and selection of an underwriter, who then purchase bonds and as a result set both the interest rates and prices on the issue. Traders are individuals in the secondary market that trade bonds among other dealers and investors.

Sales includes those who are responsible for maintaining relationships with either individual or institutional investors, such as mutual funds, pension funds, and hedge funds and banks. Research and credit analysts are charged with monitoring and reviewing issuers. They are characteristically employed by rating agencies, bond insurers, and institutional investors. Operations is the arm responsible for all of the record-keeping, order-processing, and payments related to an issue. Finally, bond counsel are lawyers that represent the legal interests of bondholders, underwriters, and issuers.

Once more the simple number of actors included in a bond issue is significant. And this is to say nothing of rating agencies, special financial consultants, bond brokers, bond insurers, and banks, all of whom add to the number of actors and complexity of the process. This should again highlight the need for prudence when deciding on a bond issue. Issuing debt is an expensive and time-consuming proposition and, therefore, should not be taken lightly or with an eye to primarily short-term benefits.

## Investors

Investors are individuals, households, or institutional entities. They are the final owners of the bond debt—the bondholders. As noted by O'Hara (2012, p. 18), "The principal characteristic of all buyers of traditional municipal securities [education bonds] is that they are subject to federal income tax so that they benefit from the tax exemption." In other words, investors often choose this vehicle because interest income is frequently exempt from both federal and state/local taxes. This is a benefit for education because it is this characteristic of the debt that makes it especially attractive to investors.

Finally, to help round out the discussion about issuing debt, the next section introduces readers to the stepwise process associated with a bond issue.

The goal of doing so is not just to provide individuals who are new to fiscal administration with a descriptive account of who is involved, but also to familiarize them with the actual process itself.

## Steps in a Bond Issue

The objective of this section is to provide novice fiscal managers with a working understanding of the bond issue process. As noted previously, this chapter is aimed at furnishing information for those who find themselves with little budgetary administration experience, but who nonetheless must make decisions or become conversant with capital acquisitions and the process of using debt to leverage institutional assets. It is also intended to prepare students whose current responsibilities intersect with fiscal administration in higher education or will do so in the future.

Following both O'Hara (2012) and Weyl and Rodgers (2006, pp. 2–3) in summative fashion, Table 9.3 incorporates both the stepwise process as a whole and a short description of each step. Readers will note that many of the components of a bond issue reflect the capital budgeting process as outlined in chapter 8.

Table 9.3 has provided a rough outline for a typical bond issue in higher education. As new budget managers engage in the process of resource allocation, it is important to become a savvy consumer of information that relates to long-term financial planning. Becoming knowledgeable about debt and institutional requirements for issuing bonds is a first step in this process.

**Table 9.3 Stepwise Process for a Bond Issue**

| Step in Bond Issue | Description |
| --- | --- |
| 1. Clearly establish the use of bond proceeds | In this step the goal is to determine if new projects or existing debt will be financed or refinanced |
| 2. Obtain approvals | The institution should seek and obtain approval from appropriate oversight bodies, i.e., state, Board of Trustees, State Governing Boards; this step should be repeated/or approvals verified after a public hearing (step 10) is conducted |
| 3. Choose a bond dealer | Often entails employing a securities firm or bank; care should be taken because this entity sets the requirements regarding process and time frame |
| 4. Craft a working group | Choose institutional professionals who will work on the bond issue, including bond counsel and investment banker; these choices can be subject to the bond dealer's requirements |
| 5. Develop timeline | A timeline for uncomplicated bond issues, especially for institutions with experience issuing debt, is generally 3–4 months |

**Table 9.3** *(Continued)*.

| Step in Bond Issue | Description |
| --- | --- |
| 6. Determine security pledge and bond structure | Institutions should establish security pledges based on whether the issue is a GO or Revenue pledge and should also determine if it will issue a variable- or fixed-rate bond |
| 7. Engage credit agencies | Institutions should seek a rating from at least one, often two, rating agencies and decide if they will use a credit enhancement such as bond insurance or a state program |
| 8. Generate and review documents | Bond issues are labor and paperwork intensive processes, and this step should focus on gathering, generating, and reviewing all necessary documents |
| 9. Conduct a tax analysis | Examine pre- and post-issue tax consequences and requirements, including the use of projects funded by tax-exempt bonds, capital campaign restrictions, and bond proceed investment |
| 10. Hold a public hearing | Place a TEFRA* Notice in a general circulation newspaper 14 days before the hearing to allow for public comment on the bond issue |
| 11. Price and market bonds | This step is the responsibility of the investment banker or underwriter, depending on whether the issue is competitive or negotiated, who will price and market the bond issue |
| 12. Close the issue | Sign all documents, verify that all reports and documents are included, and make sure that bond proceeds are delivered to the bond trustee |
| 13. Disburse proceeds | This process usually happens over time, and that does not exceed three years; proceeds are distributed based on funding needs and an established timeline for drawing on proceeds |
| 14. Deal with postclosing | Finally, the bond issue does not end with disbursement, institutions are required to follow rules around investment of bond funds, disclosures, and compliance |

*Source*: O'Hara (2012) and Weyl and Rodgers (2006, pp. 2–3).
*TEFRA stands for Tax Equity and Fiscal Responsibility Act.

## CONCLUSION

Admittedly, this chapter has provided only a concise overview of capital budgeting with regard to debt. However, this information should nonetheless provide a solid foundation from which to begin understanding the role of debt and credit ratings in the fiscal administration of institutions of higher education. In closing, a major takeaway from this chapter should be that issuing debt in the form of bonds, or even other long-term debt vehicles, is certainly a decision that institutions should not take lightly.

When deciding whether or not to issue bonds, an institution should carefully weigh the short- and long-term effects of such a decision. Because debt has become more ubiquitous in higher education capital budgeting, the need to remain vigilant regarding the tradeoffs between short- and long-run benefits and costs will become ever more important. Finally, as decisions around debt are made, special attention should be focused not only on the total amount of debt, its related service, and depreciation, but also on the impacts that new projects, building, and acquisitions will have on the operating position of the institution.

## QUESTIONS ABOUT USING DEBT AND BONDS

1. What are the primary uses of debt and/or bonds in higher education?
2. Should decision-makers be concerned with rising debt levels?
3. What are some important considerations related to issuing debt?
4. What are different types of debt available to colleges and universities?
5. Thinking broadly, how does budget philosophy matter in decisions related to using debt?

## NOTES

1. Portions of this section are adapted, with permission, from Serna (2013b, c).

2. A third rating agency is Fitch's; it is not included here because its history with rating institutions of higher education is relatively short as compared to S&P and Moody's. Additionally, Fitch's rating criteria are analogous to those provided by S&P and Moody's.

*Phase IV*

# LINKAGE, PHILOSOPHY, AND CONCLUSION

The focus of the final phase is alignment. The aspiring higher education budget manager must realize that spending decisions should align with the organization's mission, vision, goals, and strategic plan. In addition, aspiring higher education budget managers must recognize the repercussions if spending patterns do not align with the stated values of the organization. Moreover, readers are encouraged to develop their own philosophy related to fiscal administration and how their philosophy plays a role in decision-making. The practice of writing down a philosophy is essential, and this philosophy statement can serve as a tool to guide budget-related decisions.

# Chapter 10

# Budgeting and Strategic Planning

In the fiscal administration of higher education institutions, much time and energy is spent planning an institution's future trajectory. Indeed, just about every college or university maintains an office dedicated to the strategic planning function. Likewise, the planning function often includes a wide cross-section of participants including administrators, faculty, and students. However, even with all of this attention, the linkage between the strategic planning function and budgets is not always explicit or evident (Goldstein, 2012; Norris & Poulton, 1991).

In this chapter, the focus is on the development of direct feedback and planning relationships between the fiscal components of institutional operations and strategic endeavors into the future. In other words, as institutional stakeholders engage in the planning process, they must explicitly consider how each goal and its related objectives will be financed.

As just noted, the planning process provides a guide for reaching institutional goals; the budget provides a means of reaching them. Not linking the two is folly at best, and a failure of leadership at worst. Hence, this chapter considers how to accomplish this as well as related implications.

## STRATEGIC PLANNING AND INSTITUTIONAL PRIORITIES

Although strategic planning is intended as a way to guide the institution over a certain time period, it is not always clear how plans are to be achieved from a fiscal standpoint. As strategic planning covers many years at a time, planners are expected to incorporate multiple aspirational notions, attempt to predict changes in the operational environment, and provide a guide for moving forward. Hence, this process should be directly and closely related to the institution's financial standing and budgeting process (Barr & McClellan, 2011; Goldstein, 2012).

Another consideration has to do with the strategic plan as an institutional document. Arguably, most individuals on campus would point to the strategic planning document as the strategic plan itself. This, unfortunately, would be a mistake. The reason for such an assertion is that the strategic plan, if undertaken carefully, should have built-in mechanisms for change and adjustment to environmental factors; the strategic planning document is by its very nature static. That is to say, the plan should evolve as conditions evolve. A static plan in the form a single planning document that includes little in the way of flexibility is of limited practical use to the institution.

This is not to suggest that a strategic plan should be short-term or limit its aspirational views to only those things that are readily attainable or that documents should not be generated. Rather, this is to suggest that the process and plan, along with associated financing, integrate sufficient buffering from well-known and even unexpected environmental fluctuations. This requires that both strategic planning and *operational planning* are considered together. Doing so will ensure that day-to-day operational and longer-term capital financing decisions are dedicated to reaching institutional goals and objectives.

Finally, it is clearly that strategic planning requires participation from around campus and decidedly requires significant energy and resources. It is then imperative that budgetary decisions support strategic goals. Additionally, the alignment of budgetary resources sends a message about which objectives are of central concern to leaders and an institution. An old adage of budgeting and fiscal administration is: "Do not tell me what you value. Instead show me your budget and I will tell you what you value."

This simple statement acknowledges the fundamental connection between resource allocation decisions and institutional priorities. In other words, what an institution espouses as a goal is of limited concrete value if not supported by resources. In what follows, this topic is further discussed and examined, and strategies are presented for helping make this alignment more explicit.

As with any organization, higher education budget managers should be cognizant of the fact that spending patterns directly influence, and, in some situations, even determine, institutional values. Ultimately, decisions-makers at all levels need guiding principles that can ensure that resource allocation decisions are made in support of the desired values and norms of the organization.

## GUIDING PRINCIPLES

In general there are four documents within any organization that fiscal managers should use as guiding principles when monitoring spending patterns. They include

1. Mission statement: According to Yukl (2002, p. 284), a "mission statement usually describes the purpose of the organization in terms of the type of activities to be performed." A mission statement describes what an organization is attempting to do in the present. It should help to establish the operational guide for the institution to meet its long-term goals.
2. Vision statement: Whereas a mission statement's focus is the present, a vision statement provides people within an organization a view of what the institution, office, department, program, and so on is striving to become in the future. It provides a vision for the future and, when properly written, elicits excitement and stimulates individuals to apply their energy and creativity toward the end goal (Yukl, 2002, p. 284). It is at the intersection of the vision and mission statements that fiscal administration is key; the budgeting component of the process helps make day-to-day decisions into long-run realities.
3. Goals: Goals within an institution of higher education relate directly to the mission and vision statements. Educational leaders will collaboratively develop both short- and long-term goals to ensure that daily actions align with the vision (Fink & Markholt, 2011, p. 172). The long- and short-terms goals serve as a reminder that the daily actions within an organization should direct the unit toward the mission and vision statements.
4. Strategic plan: The strategic plan serves to move a unit from where it is today closer toward its vision statement over a finite amount of time. A strategic plan helps provide concrete mechanisms to reach espoused objectives. The aim of a strategic plan is to identify specific actions that will be taken within an organization over a predetermined amount of time (typically, strategic plans work in five-year increments). These specific actions, if achieved, should help move the unit closer to its vision statement and goals.

Although each of these documents is unique and serves a specific purpose, taken together they provide the budget manager with a tool to gauge the appropriateness of any and all proposed financial decisions. Ultimately, each type of revenue-generation technique or expenditure decision should align with the four documents discussed here.

Schmidtlein (1989–1990) provides a basic approach to integrated strategic planning. He suggests that each type of planning process must be directly

**Table 10.1**   **Linking Planning and Budgeting**

| Planning Type | Definition | Specific Issues |
|---|---|---|
| Strategic planning | Determining the nature of the environment in which an institution operates, assessing its internal strengths and weaknesses, and developing a "vision" of its future character given these assumptions about its emerging situation; "mission planning" | Creates a set of guidelines and assumptions that guide decision-making. Does not necessarily provide day-to-day or operational guidance. Provides ambiguous but relevant context for budgeting decisions |
| Program planning | Determining the nature of the programs needed to implement the institution's vision and the types of structures and process required to support these programs (administrative, student service, public service, academic programs, etc.) | Provides more specific guidance around programmatic offerings and decisions, but only partially includes direction on resource allocation amounts |
| Facility planning | Determining character of the physical facilities needed to implement effectively an institution's programs | Directly related to program planning but because of long-term view, can deviate significantly from current facility needs. Often political in nature, and requires long-run consideration of institutional goals, objectives, and budgets |
| Operational planning | Establishing short-range objectives, determining their relative priorities, and deciding the kinds and levels of resources to be devoted to each objective; "tactical planning" | Should take place before budget decisions are made so that a clear understanding of operational plans and goals is apparent. Serves as an implicit indicator of institutional priorities |
| Budget planning | Determining goods and services needed to implement desired programs, estimating their costs, determining potential sources of revenues, and reconciling competing claims for resources, given assumptions about revenue limitations | Often undertaken simultaneously with operational planning, but includes specific allocation amounts as related to the current year's operations |
| Issue-specific planning | Determining the policies and actions required to resolve issues affecting a specific campus function or limited set of functions (e.g., computer planning, affirmative action planning, student retention planning, or faculty development planning) | Generally, a response to external and internal pressures to react to certain, undesired situations. Usually ill-defined and hard to provide specific or appropriate funding since this type of planning is decidedly responsive rather than proactive |

*Source:* Schmidtlein (1989–1990, pp. 11–14).

linked to budgeting. For example, he notes, as have others (Sanaghan, 2009, cited in Goldstein, 2012, p. 79), that each planning type has special consider-ations that must be taken into account. Each is considered here and presented in Table 10.1 for ease of exposition.

In closing this section it is necessary to highlight and summarize a few key points:

- The strategic plan is a high-level process that should include inputs from many perspectives and stakeholders. It should set the plan for the institution into the longer-term future.
- The strategic plan must not only incorporate aspirational goals and objec-tives; it must also include mechanisms to achieve and assess these efforts. Indeed, while a twenty- or thirty-year plan may help the institution think about its very long-term positioning, they likely provide rather limited actionable plans.
- The strategic plan is closely related to the mission and vision statements, but must provide actionable steps to reach espoused goals, include funding support, and remain flexible in the face of variable environmental factors.
- Finally, the strategic plan is a higher-order guide for action. Localized dis-cussion and specifics that include stakeholders at multiple levels and other planning types will help ensure that the organization, office, department, or program are all working toward similar ends.

## LIMITATIONS SURROUNDING LINKING PLANNING AND BUDGETING

As with any organizational endeavor, linking planning and budgeting has proven difficult for at least a few reasons. This section considers three of the major impediments faced by fiscal managers when linking planning and budgets. Again, this is not a comprehensive list, but a list of commonly encountered limitations.

First is the uncertain and often variable nature of future conditions. As noted previously in the text, difficulties predicting opportunities and threats abound. Indeed, a major limitation of predicting future revenues, expendi-tures, enrollments, and so on is that the forecast will always be off by some amount. However, this does not suggest that leaders should simply wait and see.

Indeed, working with what comes up is just as important as working within those things that have been planned (Schmidtlein, 1989–1990). This is where incorporating flexibility into the planning process is a core concern. Planning should not be so rigid as to inhibit institutional and fiscal administrators from responding effectively to changing environmental factors. Conversely, the plan should not be so ill-defined that most occurrences come as a surprise.

Second is the politics of institutional decision-making. Within any large organization it is paramount to account for the distribution of power. To assume that budgeting and planning are objective affairs where rationality carries the day is folly to be sure (Wildavsky, 1973). As with any human interaction, planning and budgeting are decidedly imperfect and political processes that result from the personal beliefs, judgments, and perspectives of individuals working collectively.

The potential rigidities of formal planning processes constitute the third impediment. This differs from including flexibility in the plan by instead including flexibility into the process itself. As stated previously, the planning processes requires significant time and effort. If the process is too rigid, it may inhibit key actors from participating. This could result in the exclusion of vital perspectives or buy-ins. When central actors are not included in planning, this can often create implicit but powerful disincentives for aligning organization activities and resources to meet the institution's larger mission and vision.

## POTENTIAL CONSEQUENCES OF MISALIGNMENT

The potential for misalignment between the mission, vision, goals, and strategic plan of units and the institution in terms of actual spending patterns is great. What follows are a couple of examples of how spending patterns misalign with the mission, vision, goals, and strategic plan. However, before these examples are discussed, a pivotal question asked by Schmidtlein must be revisited: "Why has it proven so difficult to align planning and budgeting?" (Schmidtlein, 1989–1990). A likely answer has to do with the divergent timing of each process.

A planning process seeks to incorporate the input of multiple stakeholders, chart a course, and achieve aspirational objectives. A budgeting process on the other hand is generally focused on a single year or handful of years. This can set each process in a position to have one of two things occur—get things done, or get things done well. The hope is that by engaging in a deliberate and focused method of integrated budgeting and planning the two processes will fruitfully inform one another.

In fact, the danger with misalignment of budgeting and planning activities is that poor decisions fail to enable institutions to improve and better serve students. Moreover, decisions or espoused ideals that lack financial support are not, by their very nature, truly held convictions or priorities. For example, on many campuses nationwide, institutions have clearly stated that diversifying their student bodies and supporting traditional underrepresented students remain key priorities. However, when institutional budgets are compared to the rhetoric of strategic plans, resources do not appear to be directed to this goal.

Another example has to do with institutional goals around research, teaching, and service. For instance, many institutions wish to enhance their research portfolios and place more emphasis on this part of their mission and identity. And while the strategic plan for most of these institutions includes this as a goal, the budgets for these same colleges and universities show that little change is evident in terms of resource allocations. Hence, without a commensurate change in the budgeting decisions made by these institutions, it is unlikely that these goals will be met.

Finally, budget manager must use the mission, vision, goals, and strategic plan to guide decisions around fiscal allocations. A useful approach may be to understand allocation decisions as those that best serve the goals of the institution, office, program, or department under certain constraints and that take advantage of opportunities when possible. Ultimately, the best decisions occur when the decisions about planning and budgets align with the organization's mission, vision, goals, and strategic plan.

## REVISITING MISSION, VISION, GOALS, AND STRATEGIC PLANS

How often should college and university leaders revisit the organization's mission, vision, goals, and strategic plan? Unfortunately, there is not a set answer to that question. However, implicit in the question is the idea that educational leaders should regularly revisit each of the documents that are guiding institutional decision-making. The thought of using a mission statement that is over twenty years old to guide current spending decisions seems misguided, assuming the mission statement no longer reflects the current direction of the organization.

Often, new administrations will take advantage of such a change to reenvision the institution's current and future trajectories. In any event, a good rule of thumb is to examine, adjust, and reformulate planning and budgets at least every three to five years at a minimum. Not doing so can mean that the institution's budgets and plans are working at cross-purposes.

It should be noted that revisiting the mission, vision, goals, and strategic plan does not necessarily mean that these documents are going to be rewritten regularly. Instead, revisiting suggests that educational leaders will review the current mission, vision, goals, and strategic plan for the organization on a regular basis to ensure that these statements continue to reflect current institutional needs and priorities.

Another possible time for revisiting the budgeting and planning process includes reaccreditation. Colleges and universities are accredited by regional organizations. These accreditation visits typically occur every seven to ten years and would serve as an opportunity to regularly revisit the organization's mission, vision, goals, and strategic plan. In addition, as leaders prepare for accreditation visits, those within the organization can be invited to collaboratively participate in this process to ensure that each of the documents truly reflects the collective and shared aspirations of the unit and institution.

## CORRECTIVE ACTION

The next question that needs to be explored is what should be done if allocation decisions fail to align with the mission, vision, goals, and strategic plan? Two specific strategies are discussed—one focused on an individual educator who might struggle with alignment and another aimed at altering the culture and climate of the organization.

Inevitably, there will be a handful of educators that will struggle with grasping the importance of ensuring spending decisions align with the organization's mission, vision, goals, and strategic plan. Leaders working with such educators should take the time to meet with these individuals and explain why alignment is essential. Effective leaders will initiate this conversation before making a decision on the proposed expenditure. For example, it would make sense to ask individuals at each level to help explain how the proposed expenditure aligns with the mission, vision, goals, and strategic plan. When individuals are unable to do so, or the answers are not cohesive, this could suggest that clearer processes are needed.

## CONCLUSION

All educators, including educational leaders charged with overseeing and managing budgets, should recognize the importance of alignment between spending patterns and the organization's mission, vision, goals, and strategic plan. In short, alignment enables an organization to improve, whereas misalignment results in the organization staying mired in the status quo. Significant time should be put into the development of the mission, vision, goals, and strategic plan, and these documents and processes, when properly created and implemented into an organization, should collectively identify the desired direction for becoming better. By encouraging alignment of spending decisions to the mission, vision, goals, and strategic plan, budget managers will maximize the value of each dollar within the budget and support the institution in the improvement process.

## QUESTIONS AND EXERCISES FOR INTEGRATED PLANNING AND BUDGETING

1. Access the mission statement, vision statement, goals, and strategic plan of a particular institution
2. Review each of those documents
3. Access the most current budget from the same institution

Once steps 1–3 are complete, answer the following questions:

1. What are the stated values of the institution in the mission statement, vision statement, goals, and strategic plan?
2. What are the observable values of the institution based on the spending patterns reported in the budget report?
3. What do the spending patterns say about the values of the college or university?
4. How well do the values and spending decisions align?

*Chapter 11*

# Conclusion

At the beginning of this book, we introduced the idea that money is central to all that is done in public education. Then, in an effort to better illustrate the importance of proper fiscal management, we divided the discussion embedded throughout this book into four different phases. The focus of the first phase was the foundational knowledge a budget manager needs in order to effectively oversee public funds and maximize the educational opportunities of all students. Some of the pertinent topics covered in the first phase included revenues, expenditures, financial ratios, and forecasting.

In the second phase, we shifted the discussion to address the steps that higher education budget managers should take when developing and overseeing budgets. We reviewed the typical budget cycle for a higher education budget manager. Then, we reviewed concepts related to overseeing and auditing college and university budgets. We also reviewed the concept of variance analysis.

For the third phase, our discussion centered on capital budgeting. Specifically, we reviewed strategies that higher education budget managers and administrators can consider when attempting to fund capital projects either with or without debt. The aim of the fourth and final phase was to help aspiring and practicing higher education budget managers develop their own philosophy related to managing an institutional budget and to appreciate the importance of aligning spending practices to the organization's vision, mission, goals, and strategic plan.

In addition to the discussion provided throughout the book, we have attempted to provide the reader with practical examples that took the different theoretical concepts and applied them to "real-life" situations. These practical examples were, ultimately, the reason we wrote this book. We knew there were plenty of outstanding higher education finance and budgeting textbooks available. What we felt was missing for aspiring college and university budget managers was an opportunity to apply the budgetary concepts into practice. We recognize the importance of experience in the learning process, and it is our hope that the experiences provided to readers through the various exercises in this book have solidified their understanding of budgeting practices.

In conclusion, we would like to review those overarching concepts that we hope every reader gained a better understanding of and appreciation for as a result of this book:

1. *Know who to ask*—As we have stated throughout this book, we recognize that most aspiring educational leaders pursue leadership positions due to their commitment and expertise in areas such as curriculum or leadership. Very few seek leadership positions as a result of their budgetary abilities. However, it is essential for all leaders to become conversant with managing budgets.

   It is our contention that this book will lay a basic foundation that will enable aspiring higher education and student affairs leaders to, eventually, become experts in managing budgets. However, savvy leaders will continue to seek out opportunities to grow in their abilities to manage a budget. Part of growing as a budget manager includes dialoguing with others who possess greater expertise. As a result, we strongly encourage aspiring budget managers to identify who they can consult with when they have questions concerning the management of a college or university budget. Then, consult with that individual or those individuals as questions arise.

2. *Alignment*—As was discussed earlier in the book, the best budget managers at any level and in any organization should always try to align all spending decisions with the organization's vision, mission, goals, and strategic plan. Spending patterns should clearly demonstrate the values of the organization. Failure to achieve alignment results in greater inefficiency and in ineffective spending decisions. Ultimately, the failure to achieve alignment results in inferior educational opportunities for students within the organization.

3. *Transparency*—In higher education, budget managers should strive to make all money-related decisions in a transparent manner. Transparency fosters greater trust within all individuals in the organization, whereas a lack of transparency garners mistrust and apprehension. Higher education budget managers that master transparency will observe, in addition to greater trust, a greater willingness for cooperation from those within the organization. Transparency is an essential component to collaborative leadership.

4. *Collaborate*—Budget decisions should, for the most part, be made collaboratively. Educational leaders, especially in higher education where governance of the institution is diffuse, who fail to collaboratively involve others within the organization in budget decisions unintentionally jeopardize trust between the administration, faculty, and staff. Conversely, educational leaders who utilize broad-based teams and decision-making to make budgetary decisions increase the transparency around financial decisions, augment cooperation for the direction of the organization, and ensure the fiscal decisions align with the desires of the majority of stakeholders.

5. *Educate others*—Educational leaders with an expertise in budget management have a responsibility to educate other stakeholders on relevant finance and budgeting issues. For example, policymakers should understand the strains on the total program for the institution and the need for additional funding. Faculty and staff should understand how money and full-time equivalencies flow into operating revenues and how these are then allocated.

   There are too many higher education and student affairs leaders that seem to personify the "I don't really know much about finance or budgeting" attitude, and this apathy harms public education and potentially important funding to these offices and programs. Our hope is that those who read this book will have the knowledge necessary to explain finance and budget concepts and seek out opportunities to do so.

6. *Use knowledge to influence others*—Finally, we hope that this book has provided readers with the knowledge of finance and budget that will empower them to influence others. Specifically, public education desperately needs more advocates with a working understanding of financial and budgetary practices that can coherently convince state policymakers to provide public education with adequate funding.

We hope you have discovered the joy associated with effectively managing public funds in a way that maximizes the educational opportunities of each and every student within an organization. A strong understanding of budgetary practices is imperative for educational leaders seeking to promote greater educational achievement. We feel the content and exercises embedded in this book have provided the reader with the foundation necessary to maximize the power of each dollar entrusted to higher education budget managers. We look forward to hearing from readers on how the book has contributed to their abilities to effectively lead colleges, universities, offices, programs, and departments.

# References and Further Reading

Archibald, R., & Feldman, D. (2006). State Higher Education Spending and the Tax Revolt. *The Journal of Higher Education, 77* (4), 618–43.

Archibald, R., & Feldman, D. (2008). Explaining Increases in Higher Education Costs. *The Journal of Higher Education, 79* (3), 268–95.

Archibald, R., & Feldman, D. (2011). *Why Does College Cost So Much?* New York: Oxford University Press.

Barr, M., & McClellan, G. (2011). *Budgeting and Financial Management in Higher Education* (3rd ed.). San Francisco, CA: Jossey-Bass.

Bogaty, E., & Nelson, J. (2013). *Announcement: Moody's: 2013 Outlook for Entire US Higher Education Sector Changed to Negative.* New York, NY: Moody's Investor Services: Global Credit Research.

Box, G., & Jenkins, G. M. (2008). *Time Series Analysis: Forecasting and Control.* Hoboken, NJ: John Wiley & Sons, Inc.

Chabotar, K. (1989). Financial Ratio Analysis Comes to Non-Profits. *The Journal of Higher Education, 60* (2), 188–208.

Cheslock, J., & Gianneschi, M. (2008). Replacing State Appropriations with Alternative Revenue Sources: The Case of Voluntary Support. *The Journal of Higher Education, 79* (2), 208–29.

Cox, B., Weiler, S., & Cornelius, L. (2013). *The Costs of Education.* Lancaster, PA: ProActive Publications.

Daley, R. A. (2010). *Determinants of Credit Ratings for US Private Colleges and Universities, Honors Theses. Paper 576.* Retrieved March 21, 2013, from Digital Commons: Colby College: http://digitalcommons.colby.edu/honorstheses/576.

Damodaran, A. (2001). *Corporate Finance: Theory and Practice* (2nd ed.). New York, NY: John Wiley & Sons, Inc.

Damodaran, A. (2012). *Investment Analysis: Tools and Techniques for Determining the Value of Any Asset* (3rd ed.). New York, NY: Wiley: Finance.

Doty, R. (2012). *Bloomberg Visual Guide to Municipal Bonds.* Hoboken, NJ: Bloomberg Press.

Dunn, W. N. (2012). *Public Policy Analysis* (5th ed.). Upper Saddle River, NJ: Pearson.

Ely, T. (2012). Indirect Aid for Uncertain Times: The Use of State Credit Enhancement Programs. *Municipal Finance Journal, 33* (2), 61–85.

Feldstein, S., & Fabozzi, F. (2008). *The Handbook of Municipal Bonds.* Hoboken, NJ: John Wiley & Sons, Inc.

Fink, S., & Markholt, A. (2011). *Leading for Instructional Improvement: How Successful Leaders Develop Teaching and Learning Expertise.* San Francisco, CA: Jossey-Bass.

Finkler, S., Purtell, R., Calabrese, T., & Smith, D. (2013). *Financial Management for Public, Health, and Not-for-Profit Organizations* (4th ed.). Upper Saddle River, NJ: Pearson.

Fischer, M., Gordon, T., Greenlee, J., & Keating, E. (2004). Measuring Operations: An Analysis of Private College and Universities' Financial Statements. *Financial Accountability & Management, 20* (2), 129–51.

Goldstein, L. (2012). *A Guide to College & University Budgeting: Foundations for Institutional Effectiveness* (4th ed.). Washington, DC: National Association of College & University Business Officers.

Governmental Accounting Standards Board. (2006, May). *The User's Perspective.* Retrieved April 16, 2015 from Financial Statement Users: http://gasb.org/cs/ContentServer?c=GASBContent_C&pagename=GASB%2FGASBContent_C%2FUsersArticlePage&cid=1176156737123.

Hegar, G. (2015, July 2). *Liabilities Payable from Restricted Assets.* Retrieved September 18, 2015, from Reporting Requirements for Fiscal Year 2015: Annual Financial Reports of State Agencies and Universities: https://fmx.cpa.state.tx.us/fmx/pubs/afrrptreq/notes/index.php?menu=1&section=note5&page=liabilities_payable.

Heller, D. (2006). State Support of Higher Education: Past, Present, and Future. In D. Priest, & E. St. John (Eds.), *Privatization and Public Universities.* Bloomington, IN: Indiana University Press.

Heller, D. (2011). Trends in the Affordability of Public Colleges and Universities: The Contradiction of Increasing Prices and Increasing Enrollment. In D. Heller (Ed.), *The States and Public Higher Education Policy: Affordability, Access, and Accountability.* Baltimore, MD: The Johns Hopkins University Press.

Hillman, N., Tandberg, D., & Gross, J. (2014). Performance Funding in Higher Education: Do Financial Incentives Impact College Completions? *The Journal of Higher Education, 85* (6), 826–57.

Inside Higher Ed. (2013, January 4). *Moody's: Higher Ed Downgrades Vastly Exceeded Upgrades in 2012.* Retrieved March 20, 2013, from Inside Higher Ed: http://www.insidehighered.com/quicktakes/2013/02/04/moodys-higher-ed-downgrades-vastly-exceeded-upgrades-2012#.URCjtlwYQok.mailto.

Jacob, B., McCall, B., & Stange, K. (2013). *College as Country Club: Do Colleges Cater to Students' Preferences for Consumption.* Cambridge, MA: National Bureau of Economic Research.

Kalsbeek, D., & Hossler, D. (2008). Enrollment Management a Market-Center Perspective. *College & University, 84* (3), 2–11.

Key Jr., V. O. (1940). The Lack of a Budgetary Theory. *American Political Science Review, 34* (6), 1137–44.

Kirp, D. (2003). *Shakespeare, Einstein & the Bottom Line: The Marketing of Higher Education.* Cambridge, MA: Harvard University Press.

Kosten, L., & Lovell, C. (2011). Academic Deans' Perspective on the Effectiveness of Responsibility Centered Management. In C. Rylee, *Integrated Resource and Budget Planning at Colleges and Universities* (pp. 85–101). Ann Arbor, MI: Society for College and University Planning.

Lee Jr., R., Johnson, R., & Joyce, P. (2013). *Public Budgeting Systems* (9th ed.). Burlington, MA: Jones & Bartlett Learning.

Lerner, J., Schoar, A., & Wang, J. (2008). Secrets of the Academy: The Drivers of University Endowment Success. *The Journal of Economic Perspectives, 22* (3), 207–22.

Lowry, R. (2001). The Effects of State Political Interests and Campus Outputs on Public University Revenues. *Economics of Education Review, 20,* 105–19.

McKeown-Moak, M., & Mullin, C. (2014). *Higher Education Finance Research: Policy, Politics, and Practice.* Charlotte, NC: Information Age Publishing.

McLendon, M., Hearn, J., & Deaton, R. (2006). Called to Account: Analyzing the Origins and Spread of State Performance-Accountability Policies for Higher Education. *Educational Evaluation and Policy Analysis, 28* (1), 1–24.

McLendon, M., Hearn, J., & Mokher, C. (2009). Partisans, Professionals, and Power: The Role of Political Factors in State Higher Education Funding. *The Journal of Higher Education, 80* (6), 686–713.

Mincke, B. (2008). How to Analyze Higher Education Bonds. In S. Feldstein, & F. Fabozzi, *The Handbook of Municipal Bonds.* Hoboken, NJ: John Wiley & Sons, Inc.

Moody's. (2013). *US Higher Education Outlook Negative in 2013: Revenue Pressure on All Fronts Intensifies Need to Grapple with Traditional Cost Structure.* New York, NY: Moody's Investor Services.

Murnane, R., & Willett, J. (2011). *Methods Matter: Improving Causal Inference in Educational and Social Science Research.* New York, NY: Oxford University Press.

National Center for Educational Statistics. (2010). *Public Elementary and Secondary Students, Schools, Pupil/Teacher rations, and Finances, by Type of Locale: 2007–2008 and 2008–2009.* From http://nces.ed.gov/programs/digest/d10/tables/dt10_093.asp.

National Center for Educational Statistics. (2011). *Revenues and Expenditures for Public Elementary and Secondary Education: School Year 2008–2009 (Fiscal Year 2009).* From http://nces.edu.gov/pubs2011/expenditures/tables/table_01.asp.

Norris, D., & Poulton, N. (1991). *A Guide for New Planners.* Ann Arbor, MI: Society for College and University Planning (SCUP).

Odden, A., & Picus, L. (2008). *School Finance: A Policy Perspective* (4th ed.). Boston, MA: McGraw Hill.

O'Hara, N. (2012). *The Fundamental of Municipal Bonds* (6th ed.). Hoboken, NJ: Securities Industry and Financial Markets Association; John Wiley & Sons, Inc.: Wiley Finance.

O'Loughlin, E. (2012, September 25). *How to Draw a Basic Control Chart in Excel 2010*. Retrieved August 10, 2014, from https://www.youtube.com/watch?v=zvp8qmH3Eos.

Pamley, K., Bell, A., L'Orange, H., & Lingenfelter. (2009). *State Budgeting for Higher Education in the United States: As Reported for Fiscal Year 2007*. Boulder, CO: State Higher Education Executive Officers.

Parkin, M. (2010). *Microeconmics* (9th ed.). Upper Saddle River, NJ: Prentice Hall.

Prager, McCarthy, & Sealy, L. L. C. (2002). *Ratio Analysis in Higher Education: New Insights for Leaders of Public Higher Education* (5th ed.). Amstelveen, Netherlands: KPMG LLP.

Rylee, C. (2011). Introduction and Overview. In C. Rylee, *Integrated Budgeting and Planning at Colleges and Universities* (p. 1). Ann Arbor, MI: Society for College and University Planning.

SAS/STAT (R). (2009). *User's Guide*. Retrieved August 6, 2014, from Mean Squared Error: http://support.sas.com/documentation/cdl/en/statug/63033/HTML/default/viewer.htm#statug_intromod_sect005.htm.

Schmidtlein, F. (1989–1990). Why Linking Budgets to Plans has Proven Difficult in Higher Education. *Planning for Higher Education, 18* (2), 9–24.

Serna, G. R. (2013a). Understanding the Effects of State Oversight and Fiscal Policy on University Revenues: Considerations for Financial Planning. *Planning for Higher Education, 41* (2), 1–16.

Serna, G. R. (2013b). Employing College and University Credit Ratings as Indicators of Institutional Planning Effectiveness. *Planning for Higher Education, 41* (4), 1–11.

Serna, G. R. (2013c). Rating Public Colleges and Universities: Process, Practice, and Implications for Finance, Administration, and Policy. *Journal of Higher Education Management, 28* (1), 52–69.

Serna, G. R., & Weiler, S. (2014). State of the States Update: Colorado. *Journal of Education Finance, 39* (3), 250–52.

Serna, G. R. (2015). Do Tax Revolt Provisions Influence Tuition and Fee Levels? Evidence from the States using Recent Panel Data. *Journal of Education Finance, 41* (1), 48–82.

St. John, E., & Priest, D. (2006). Privatization in Public Universities. In D. Priest, & E. St. John (Eds.), *Privatization and Public Universities*. Bloomington, IN: Indiana University Press.

Standard & Poor's. (2013). *U.S. Higher Education Sector Could Experience a Rise in Rating and Outlook Changes in 2013*. San Francisco, CA: Standard & Poor's Rating Services: RatingsDirect.

Stevenson, W. (2015). *Operations Management* (12th ed.). New York: McGraw-Hill.

Tandberg, D. (2008). The Politics of Higher Education Funding. *Higher Education in Review, 5*, 1–36.

Tandberg, D., & Hillman, N. (2014). State Higher Education Performance Funding: Data, Outcomes, and Policy Implications. *Journal of Education Finance, 39* (3), 222–43.

Terenzini, P. (Winter 1999). On the Nature of Institutional Research and the Knowledge and Skills It Requires. *New Directions in Institutional Research, 104*, 21–29.

Thelin, J. (2004). Higher Education and the Public Trough. In E. St. John, & M. Parsons (Eds.), *Public Funding of Higher Education: Changing Contexts and New Rationales.* Baltimore, MC: The Johns Hopkins University Press.

Toutkoushian, R. (2001). Trends in Revenues and Expenditures for Public and Private Universities. In M. Paulsen, & J. Smart, *The Finance of Higher Education: Theory, Research, Policy & Practice* (pp. 11–38). New York, NY: Agathon Press.

Toutkoushian, R. (2003). Weathering the storm: Generating Revenues for Higher Education During a Recession. In F. Alexander, & R. Ehrenberg (Eds.), *Maximizing Revenue for Higher Education* (pp. 27–40). San Francisco, CA: Josey-Bass.

Trochim, W., & Donnelly, J. (2007). *The Research Methods Knowledge Base* (3rd ed.). Boston, MA: Cengage.

Varlotta, L. (2010). Becoming a Leader in University Budgeting. In L. Varlotta, & B. Jones, *Student Affairs Budgeting and Financial Management in the Midst of Financial Crisis* (pp. 5–20). Hoboken, NJ: Josey-Bass: An Imprint of Wiley.

Vernier: Tech Info Library. (2011, October 18). *What are Mean Squared Error and Root Mean Squared Error?* Retrieved August 6, 2014, from http://www.vernier.com/til/1014/.

Weyl, S., & Rodgers, R. (2006). *Tax-Exempt Bonds: Considerations for College and University Counsel.* Washington, DC: National Association of College and University Attorneys.

Wildavsky, A. (1978). A Budget for All Seasons? Why the Traditional Budget Lasts. *Public Administration Review, 38* (6), 501–9.

Wildavsky, A. (1973). If Planning Is Everything, Maybe It's Nothing. *Policy Sciences, 4* (2), 127–53.

Winston, G. (1999). Subsidies, Hierarchy and Peers: The Awkward Economics of Higher Education. *Journal of Economic Perspectives, 13* (1), 13–36.

Yukl, G. (2002). *Leadership in Organizations* (5th ed.). Upper Saddle River, NJ: Prentice Hall.

# Index

# About the Authors

**Dr. Gabriel R. Serna** has nearly thirteen years of experience in higher education. This includes his tenure as director of programming at New Mexico State University, as assistant director of admissions at the University of Kentucky, as associate instructor at Indiana University Bloomington, as assistant professor in the Higher Education and Student Affairs Leadership program at the University of Northern Colorado, and currently as assistant professor in the School of Education at Virginia Tech. Dr. Serna's research interests lie in the areas of higher education economics, finance, and policy. He is particularly interested in the economic relationships between states and their public institutions, student price-response, college and university fiscal administration, and enrollment management. Some of his published work can be seen in the *Journal of Education Finance,* the *Journal of Higher Education Management,* the *Planning for Higher Education Journal,* the *Handbook of Strategic Enrollment Management,* and the *Encyclopedia of Education Economics & Finance.* Additionally, Dr. Serna's research was nationally recognized by the *Journal of Education Finance* and by the National Education Finance Academy with the "Outstanding Article of the Year" award in 2015. He also serves on the editorial boards of the ASHE Report Series, Research in Higher Education, and the Journal of College & Character. Dr. Serna earned his BBA in Economics from New Mexico State University, MPP in public finance & budgeting from the Martin School of Public Policy & Administration at the University of Kentucky, and his PhD in education policy from Indiana University Bloomington.

**Dr. Spencer C. Weiler** worked in public education as both a history teacher and an assistant principal in Utah and Virginia for fifteen years. After completing his doctoral studies at Virginia Tech with an emphasis on school finance and school law, Dr. Weiler came to the University of Northern Colorado in 2007. Although Dr. Weiler genuinely misses the energy and enthusiasm unique to public schools and working directly with students, he is honored to instill in aspiring educational leaders an understanding of school finance and budget processes. Dr. Weiler strives to use his research to ensure that all students have an appropriate access to education. He has coauthored one book and authored seven book chapters and over fifteen journal articles in *Journal of Education Finance, Brigham Young University Education Law Journal, Educational Considerations, Journal of International Education and Leadership, Equity and Excellence in Education, Planning and Change,* and *West's Education Law Reporter.*

Made in the USA
Monee, IL
27 January 2020